French
Grammar

WITHDRAWN

French
Grammar

WILLIAM ROWLINSON

OXFORD
UNIVERSITY PRESS

OXFORD
UNIVERSITY PRESS

Great Clarendon Street, Oxford OX2 6DP

Oxford University Press is a department of the University of Oxford.
It furthers the University's objective of excellence in research, scholarship,
and education by publishing worldwide in

Oxford New York

Athens Auckland Bangkok Bogotá Buenos Aires Calcutta
Cape Town Chennai Dar es Salaam Delhi Florence Hong Kong Istanbul
Karachi Kuala Lumpur Madrid Melbourne Mexico City Mumbai
Nairobi Paris São Paulo Singapore Taipei Tokyo Toronto Warsaw

with associated companies in Berlin Ibadan

Oxford is a registered trade mark of Oxford University Press
in the UK and in certain other countries

Published in the United States
by Oxford University Press Inc., New York

British Library Cataloguing in Publication Data

Data available

Library of Congress Cataloging in Publication Data

Data available

ISBN 0-19-860341-X

10 9 8 7 6 5 4 3 2 1

Printed in Great Britain by
Mackays of Chatham plc, Chatham, Kent

| Introduction

This French Grammar is more thorough and more practical than other paperback grammars. It is also more up to date. In the next 300 pages you will find:

■ All the basic grammar of French presented clearly, comprehensively, and succinctly.

■ Explanations that use everyday language, and a glossary of absolutely all the grammatical terms we have used.

■ Up-to-date explanations of modern French usage not found in other grammars of this size.

■ Short, simple, easy-to-follow French examples for points of basic grammar, and longer examples from modern French sources where they are needed to explain usage.

■ A clear layout.

This grammar is *really* comprehensive. It will explain problems met by beginners, it will be a reliable learning aid for GCSE and A level, and it will remain a first resource for quick reference and revision for French specialists who have reached university and polytechnic level. As well as covering all the grammar used in modern French, it has sections on translation problems and pronunciation traps, verb tables with the conjugation of more than a hundred irregular verbs, an alphabetical list of French prepositions and their use, sections on word order and punctuation, a glossary of grammatical terms and an easy-to-use index.

Acknowledgements

The author wishes to thank Micheline Windsor, Natalie Pomier, and Laurence Delacroix for their help, and the editorial staff of Oxford University Press for their usual unfailing support, advice, and encouragement.

Contents

Verbs

TENSE FORMATION

The tenses of French verbs are either *simple*, in which
case the verb is a single word, or *compound*, in which case
it is normally formed from a part of the verb **avoir**, *to
have*, followed by the past participle:

> simple tense: **je porte**, *I wear*
> compound tense: **j'ai porté**, *I have worn*

Regular verbs, what they are

Most French verbs are regular—that is they follow an
entirely predictable pattern. The pattern they follow is
determined by the way their infinitive ends. They divide
into three groups (known as conjugations), each with its
own infinitive ending:

> port**er**, *to wear*, first conjugation
> fin**ir**, *to finish*, second conjugation
> vend**re**, *to sell*, third conjugation

Most French verbs belong to the first conjugation,
whose infinitives all end in **-er**. All invented new verbs
are automatically first conjugation verbs. Verbs in the
second conjugation all have an infinitive ending **-ir**, and
those in the very small third conjugation all have an
infinitive ending **-re**.

Irregular verbs, what they are

Some French verbs are irregular, following no pattern.
In the simple tenses there is no way of predicting their

stems (the part of the verb to which endings are added)
or, quite frequently, the endings that are added to them.
In the compound tenses, however, it is only the past
participle which is irregular. So, for example, with
vouloir (irregular), *to want*:

present (*simple tense*)   *perfect* (*compound tense*)

je veux	**j'ai voulu**
tu veux	**tu as voulu**
il veut	**il a voulu**
nous voulons	**nous avons voulu**
vous voulez	**vous avez voulu**
ils veulent	**ils ont voulu**

▶ There is a table of all the common irregular verbs
with their conjugation on page 242.

Simple-tense formation, regular verbs

To form each simple tense a fixed set of endings is added
to the verb's stem. The stem is the infinitive minus its
-er, **-ir** or **-re** ending. Each conjugation has a different
set of verb endings.

> **porter** → **port-** → **je** porte, *I wear*
> **finir** → **fin-** → **je** finis, *I finish*
> **vendre** → **vend-** → **je** vends, *I sell*

The ending of the verb corresponds to the subject of
the verb:

> **je** finis, *I finish*
> **il** finit, *he finishes*

▶ The complete tense-formation of regular verbs is
given on pp. 4–12, with the verb endings printed in bold.

Compound-tense formation, all verbs

To form a compound tense you need to know a verb's
past participle. The past participle of a regular verb is

formed by removing the **-er**, **-ir**, or **-re** of the infinitive. To this stem is added **-é** (first conjugation), **-i** (second conjugation), or **-u** (third conjugation):

infinitive		*past participle*
porter	→	porté
finir	→	fini
vendre	→	vendu

The tenses of **avoir** used to form the compound tenses are:

> perfect tense:
> present of **avoir**: j'**ai** porté
>
> pluperfect tense:
> imperfect of **avoir**: j'**avais** porté
>
> future perfect tense:
> future of **avoir**: j'**aurai** porté
>
> conditional perfect tense:
> conditional of **avoir**: j'**aurais** porté
>
> past anterior tense:
> past historic of **avoir**: j'**eus** porté
>
> perfect subjunctive:
> present subjunctive of **avoir**: j'**aie** porté
>
> pluperfect subjunctive:
> imperfect subjunctive of **avoir**: j'**eusse** porté

▶ Some very common French verbs form their compound tenses with **être** instead of **avoir**. See p. 12.

▶ In all the compound tenses the past participle may sometimes agree with its subject or its direct object, in gender and in number. See p. 14.

CONJUGATION OF -er VERBS

(First-conjugation verbs)

In all tenses **elle** (*she*), **on** (*one*) and singular nouns are followed by the **il** form of the verb; **elles** (*they*, feminine) and plural nouns are followed by the **ils** form of the verb.

infinitive	**porter**, *to wear*
present participle	**portant**, *wearing*
past participle	**porté**, *worn*
imperative	**porte**, *wear…!*
	portons, *let's wear…*
	portez, *wear…!*

Simple tenses

present tense,	je port**e**	nous port**ons**
I wear, I am wearing	tu port**es**	vous port**ez**
	il port**e**	ils port**ent**
imperfect tense,	je port**ais**	nous port**ions**
I wore, I was wearing,	tu port**ais**	vous port**icz**
I used to wear	il port**ait**	ils port**aient**
past historic tense,	je port**ai**	nous port**âmes**
I wore	tu port**as**	vous port**âtes**
	il port**a**	ils port**èrent**
future tense,	je port**erai**	nous port**erons**
I shall wear, I shall	tu port**eras**	vous port**erez**
be wearing	il port**era**	ils port**eront**
conditional tense,	je port**erais**	nous port**erions**
I should wear	tu port**erais**	vous port**eriez**
	il port**erait**	ils port**eraient**
present subjunctive,	je port**e**	nous port**ions**
I wear, I may wear	tu port**es**	vous port**iez**
	il port**e**	ils port**ent**
imperfect subjunctive*,	je port**asse**	nous port**assions**
I wore, I might wear	tu port**asses**	vous port**assiez**
	il port**ât**	ils port**assent**

* archaic or literary

Compound tenses

perfect tense,	j'**ai** porté	nous **avons** porté
I wore, I have worn,	tu **as** porté	vous **avez** porté
I have been wearing	il **a** porté	ils **ont** porté

pluperfect tense,	j'**avais** porté	nous **avions** porté
I had worn, I had	tu **avais** porté	vous **aviez** porte
been wearing	il **avait** porté	ils **avaient** porté

future perfect tense,	j'**aurai** porté	nous **aurons** porté
I shall have worn, I	tu **auras** porté	vous **aurez** porté
shall have been	il **aura** porté	ils **auront** porté
wearing		

conditional perfect	j'**aurais** porté	nous **aurions** porté
tense, I should	tu **aurais** porté	vous **auriez** porté
have worn	il **aurait** porté	ils **auraient** porté

past anterior tense*,	j'**eus** porté	nous **eûmes** porté
I had worn	tu **eus** porté	vous **eûtes** porté
	il **eut** porté	ils **eurent** porté

perfect subjunctive,	j'**aie** porté	nous **ayons** porté
I wore, I may	tu **aies** porté	vous **ayez** porté
have worn	il **ait** porté	ils **aient** porté

pluperfect	j'**eusse** porté	nous **eussions** porté
subjunctive*, I	tu **eusses** porté	vous **eussiez** porté
had worn	il **eût** porté	ils **eussent** porté

Imperative of -er verbs

The **tu** form of the imperative of **-er** verbs (also verbs like **ouvrir**, see p. 29) has no **-s** except when followed by **y** or **en**:

> **donne-le-moi!**, *give it to me!*
> **donnes-en à ta sœur aussi!**, *give your sister some as well!*
> **vas-y!**, *go on!*

* archaic or literary

Spelling changes in some -er verbs

▶ Tenses with changes are given in detail in the verb tables on p. 239.

■ Verbs ending **-e[CONSONANT]er** change the **e** of the stem to **è** when a silent **e** follows:

mener → **je mène**

They also make this change in the future and conditional, where the **e** that follows is soft rather than silent:

je mènerai; je mènerais

■ verbs ending **-eter** and **-eler**, however, usually produce the open sound in the **e** by doubling the consonant:

jeter → **je jette**
rappeler → **je rappelle**

■ some verbs ending **-eter** and **-eler** follow the pattern of **mener**, changing the **e** to **è**:

acheter → **j'achète**
geler → **je gèle**

Most verbs that do this are, however, quite uncommon. The only ones you are at all likely to encounter are:

acheter, *buy*	**geler,** *freeze*
ciseler, *engrave*	**haleter,** *pant*
congeler, *(deep) freeze*	**modeler,** *model*
crocheter, *hook (up)*	**peler,** *peel*
déceler, *disclose*	**racheter,** *buy back,*
dégeler, *thaw*	*buy again*
démanteler, dismantle	

■ Verbs ending **-é[CONSONANT]er** change the **é** to **è** before a silent **e** in the same way, *except in the future and conditional tenses:*

espérer → **j'espère**, but
j'espérerai; j'espérerais

■ Verbs ending **-cer** and **-ger** change the **c** to **ç** and the **g** to **ge** before **a** and **o**. This keeps the **c** and the **g** soft:

commencer → **nous commençons**
manger → **nous mangeons**

■ Verbs ending **-oyer** and **-uyer** change the **y** to **i** before a silent **e**:

envoyer → **j'envoie**
appuyer → **j'appuie**

With verbs ending **-ayer** this change is optional:

payer → **je paie** or **je paye**

CONJUGATION OF -ir VERBS

(Second-conjugation verbs)

In all tenses **elle** (*she*), **on** (*one*), and singular nouns are followed by the **il** form of the verb; **elles** (*they*, feminine) and plural nouns are followed by the **ils** form of the verb.

infinitive	fin**ir**, *to finish*
present participle	fin**issant**, *finishing*
past participle	fin**i**, *finished*
imperative	fin**is**, *finish …!*
	fin**issons**, *let's finish …*
	fin**issez**, *finish …!*

Simple tenses

present tense,	je fin**is**	nous fin**issons**
I finish, I am	tu fin**is**	vous fin**issez**
finishing	il fin**it**	ils fin**issent**

imperfect tense, I finished, I was finishing, I used to finish	je fin**issais** tu fin**issais** il fin**issait**	nous fin**issions** vous fin**issiez** ils fin**issaient**
past historic tense, I finished	je fin**is** tu fin**is** il fin**it**	nous fin**îmes** vous fin**îtes** ils fin**irent**
future tense, I shall finish, I shall be finishing	je fin**irai** tu fin**iras** il fin**ira**	nous fin**irons** vous fin**irez** ils fin**iront**
conditional tense, I should finish	je fin**irais** tu fin**irais** il fin**irait**	nous fin**irions** vous fin**iriez** ils fin**iraient**
present subjunctive, I finish, I may finish	je fin**isse** tu fin**isses** il fin**isse**	nous fin**issions** vous fin**issiez** ils fin**issent**
imperfect subjunctive*, I finished, I might finish	je fin**isse** tu fin**isses** il fin**ît**	nous fin**issions** vous fin**issiez** ils fin**issent**

Compound tenses

perfect tense, I finished, I have finished	j'**ai** fini tu **as** fini il **a** fini	nous **avons** fini vous **avez** fini ils **ont** fini
pluperfect tense, I had finished	j'**avais** fini tu **avais** fini il **avait** fini	nous **avions** fini vous **aviez** fini ils **avaient** fini
future perfect tense, I shall have finished	j'**aurai** fini tu **auras** fini il **aura** fini	nous **aurons** fini vous **aurez** fini ils **auront** fini
conditional perfect tense, I should have finished	j'**aurais** fini tu **aurais** fini il **aurait** fini	nous **aurions** fini vous **auriez** fini ils **auraient** fini

* archaic or literary

past anterior tense*, *I had finished*	j'**eus** fini	nous **eûmes** fini
	tu **eus** fini	vous **eûtes** fini
	il **eut** fini	ils **eurent** fini
perfect subjunctive, *I finished, I may have finished*	j'**ale** fini	nous **ayons** fini
	tu **ales** fini	vous **ayez** fini
	il **ait** fini	ils **alent** fini
pluperfect subjunctive*, *I had finished*	j'**eusse** fini	nous **eussions** fini
	tu **eusses** fini	vous **eussiez** fini
	il **eût** fini	ils **eussent** fini

CONJUGATION OF -re VERBS

(Third-conjugation verbs)

In all tenses **elle** (*she*), **on** (*one*), and singular nouns are followed by the **il** form of the verb; **elles** (*they*, feminine) and plural nouns are followed by the **ils** form of the verb.

infinitive	ven**dre**, *to sell*
present participle	vend**ant**, *selling*
past participle	vend**u**, *sold*
imperative	vend**s**, *sell ...!*
	vend**ons**, *let's sell ...*
	vend**ez**, *sell ...!*

Simple tenses

present tense, *I sell, I am selling*	je vend**s**	nous vend**ons**
	tu vend**s**	vous vend**ez**
	il vend	ils vend**ent**
imperfect tense, *I sold, I was selling, I used to sell*	je vend**ais**	nous vend**ions**
	tu vend**ais**	vous vend**iez**
	il vend**ait**	ils vend**aient**

* archaic or literary

past historic tense, *I sold*	je vend**is**	nous vend**îmes**
	tu vend**is**	vous vend**îtes**
	il vend**it**	ils vend**irent**
future tense, *I shall sell, I shall* *be selling*	je vend**rai**	nous vend**rons**
	tu vend**ras**	vous vend**rez**
	il vend**ra**	ils vend**ront**
conditional tense, *I should sell*	je vend**rais**	nous vend**rions**
	tu vend**rais**	vous vend**riez**
	il vend**rait**	ils vend**raient**
present subjunctive, *I sell, I may sell*	je vend**e**	nous vend**ions**
	tu vend**es**	vous vend**iez**
	il vend**e**	ils vend**ent**
imperfect subjunctive*, *I sold, I might sell*	je vend**isse**	nous vend**issions**
	tu vend**isses**	vous vend**issiez**
	il vend**ît**	ils vend**issent**

Compound tenses

perfect tense, *I sold, I have sold,* *I have been selling*	j'**ai** vendu	nous **avons** vendu
	tu **as** vendu	vous **avez** vendu
	il **a** vendu	ils **ont** vendu
pluperfect tense, *I had sold, I had* *been selling*	j'**avais** vendu	nous **avions** vendu
	tu **avais** vendu	vous **aviez** vendu
	il **avait** vendu	ils **avaient** vendu
future perfect tense, *I shall have sold*	j'**aurai** vendu	nous **aurons** vendu
	tu **auras** vendu	vous **aurez** vendu
	il **aura** vendu	ils **auront** vendu
conditional perfect tense, *I should* *have sold*	j'**aurais** vendu	nous **aurions** vendu
	tu **aurais** vendu	vous **auriez** vendu
	il **aurait** vendu	ils **auraient** vendu
past anterior tense*, *I had sold*	j'**eus** vendu	nous **eûmes** vendu
	tu **eus** vendu	vous **eûtes** vendu
	il **eut** vendu	ils **eurent** vendu

* archaic or literary

| perfect subjunctive,
  I sold, I may have
  sold | j'**aie** vendu
tu **aies** vendu
il **ait** vendu | nous **ayons** vendu
vous **ayez** vendu
ils **aient** vendu |
| pluperfect
  subjunctive*,
  I had sold | j'**eusse** vendu
tu **eusses** vendu
il **eût** vendu | nous **eussions** vendu
vous **eussiez** vendu
ils **eussent** vendu |

COMPOUND TENSES

▶ For the formation of the compound tenses see p. 3.

Compound tenses formed with être

Although most verbs form their compound tenses with **avoir** as the auxiliary, two groups form these tenses with **être**: reflexive verbs and a small number of common verbs expressing motion or change of state.

■ Reflexive verbs

> **je me suis levé de bonne heure**, *I got up early*
> **tu t'étais couché tard?**, *you'd gone to bed late?*

▶ See p. 30 for the formation of reflexive verbs and p. 15 for their agreement.

■ 'Motion' verbs

This is a group of thirteen common (and a few more quite uncommon) verbs mainly expressing some kind of motion or change of state, and all intransitive (used without a direct object):

arriver, *arrive*	il est arrivé
partir, *set off*	il est parti
entrer, *enter*	il est entré
sortir, *go out*	il est sorti
aller, *go*	il est allé
venir, *come*	il est venu

* archaic or literary

monter, *go up*¹	**il est monté**
descendre, *go down*	**il est descendu**
mourir, *die*	**il est mort**
naître, *be born*	**il est né**
rester, *stay*	**il est resté**
tomber, *fall*	**il est tombé**
retourner, *return*	**il est retourné**

Accourir and **passer** used intransitively may take either **être** or **avoir**:

> **elle est accourue/elle a accouru**, *she ran up*

Except **convenir à** (*suit*), all compound verbs based on the above verbs also take **être** when used intransitively.

> **je suis parvenu à le faire**, *I managed to do it*
> **il est devenu soldat**, *he became a soldier*
but   **cela ne lui a pas convenu**, *it didn't suit him*

▶ See p. 15 for the past-participle agreement with this group of verbs.

■ 'Motion' verbs used transitively

Some of the above verbs can also be used with a direct object (transitively). These verbs are:

> **descendre**, *to take down, to get down, to go down*
> **monter**, *to take up, to put up, to bring up, to go up*
> **entrer** (or more usually its compound, **rentrer**), *to
>   put in, to let in, to bring in*
> **retourner**, *to turn (over)*
> **sortir**, *to take out, to bring out*

When they are used this way they take **avoir**, not **être**:

> **il a sorti un billet de cent francs de son
>   portefeuille**, *he took a hundred-franc note from
>   his wallet*
> **j'ai descendu l'escalier**, *I came down the stairs*

■ Verbs of motion and change of state other than those listed above always take **avoir**, whether used transitively or intransitively.

> **tu as beaucoup changé,** *you've changed a lot*

Past-participle agreement in compound tenses

■ Verbs conjugated with **avoir**

In most cases the past participle of a verb conjugated with **avoir** does not change at all. However, if an **avoir** verb has a direct object, and this precedes the verb, the past participle agrees with that object in gender and number, adding **-e** for feminine singular, **-s** for masculine plural and **-es** for feminine plural.

> **tes papiers, je les ai trouvés,** *those papers of yours, I found them*
> – agreement, because direct object **les** precedes the verb
> **voilà les papiers que tu as cherchés toute la matinée,** *there are the papers you've been looking for all morning*
> – agreement, because direct object **que**, referring to **les papiers**, precedes
> **quelle date as-tu choisie?,** *what date did you choose?*
> – agreement, because direct object **quelle date** precedes

Notice that there is no agreement with an indirect object, or with **en**, or with a direct object that does not precede the verb:

> **j'ai trouvé les papiers,** *I've found the papers*
> – no agreement, direct object **les papiers** follows

c'est à Sylvie que j'ai envoyé cet argent, *it's Sylvie I sent that money to*
 – no agreement with **que**: it is the indirect object, standing for **à Sylvie**. The direct object **cet argent** follows.

les gâteaux? J'en ai mangé deux, *the cakes? I've eaten two of them*
 – no agreement with **en**: it is not a true direct object

■ Verbs conjugated with **être**

□ Intransitive verbs of motion and change of state

The past participles of the thirteen 'motion' verbs and their compounds conjugated with **être** (see p. 12) agree with the subject in gender and number, adding **-e** for feminine singular, **-s** for masculine plural, **-es** for feminine plural:

> **elle est arrivée hier**, *she arrived yesterday*
> **elles étaient parties bien avant midi**, *they'd set off long before twelve o'clock*
> **ils seront déjà sortis**, *they'll already have gone out*

□ Reflexive verbs

The past participles of reflexive verbs agree in gender and number with the preceding direct object, which in most cases will correspond to the subject:

> **elle s'est levée tard**, *she got up late*
> **ils se sont dépêchés**, *they hurried*

In some cases, however, the reflexive is an indirect object, and then there is no agreement:

> **elle s'est dit, « pourquoi pas? »**, *she said to herself, why not?*
> **ils se sont écrit toutes les semaines**, *they wrote to each other every week*

> **elle s'est cassé la cheville**, *she broke her ankle*
> – **la cheville**, the ankle, is the direct object, **se** is
> an indirect object indicating whose ankle she
> broke

but notice:

> **quelle cheville s'est-il cassée?**, *which ankle has
> he broken?*
> – the agreement is with **quelle cheville**, which is
> the direct object, precedes, and is feminine.

■ Past participle used as an adjective

The past participle may also be used simply as an
adjective, in which case, like any other adjective, it agrees
with its noun:

> **elles sont épuisées mais contentes**, *they are
> exhausted but happy*

▶ See p. 38 for all the uses of the past participle.

USE OF TENSES

The present tense

French has only one form of the present tense,
corresponding to both the present simple and the present
continuous in English. So **je mange** translates both *I eat*
and *I am eating*. There is no possible translation of *I am
eating* using the present participle in French. If the
continuing nature of the action needs to be stressed, **être
en train de** is used:

> **mais je suis en train de déjeuner!**, *but I'm still
> eating my lunch!*

General uses of the present tense

■ As in English, the present is used not just to indicate
what is going on at the moment:

je mange un œuf, *I'm eating an egg*

but also what habitually occurs:

je mange toujours un œuf au petit déjeuner,
I always have an egg for breakfast

■ It can also be used, again as in English, to indicate a future:

tu veux un œuf?, *are you having (going to have) an egg?*

■ The present tense is used much more frequently than in English to narrate a past series of events, not just in spoken French but in written French also:

1945. A Hiroshima, la bombe explose. Toute discussion est terminée … *1945. In Hiroshima, the bomb exploded. All discussion was over*

This is called the historic present, and it is used to give more immediacy to past events. But see also p. 22.

Special uses of the present tense

■ Present tense with **depuis** (*for*), **depuis que** (*since*), **voilà … que** (*since/for*) and **il y a … que** (*since/for*)

□ **Depuis, depuis que**

With the preposition **depuis** and after the conjunction **depuis que** a French present tense is used where in English we should expect a perfect:

je suis ici depuis deux jours, *I've been here (for) two days*

je le vois beaucoup plus souvent depuis que sa femme est partie, *I've seen him a lot more often since his wife's gone*

With **depuis** plus a negative, however, the tense is the same as in English:

> **je ne l'ai pas vu depuis deux jours**, *I haven't seen him for two days*

And where the action is already completed the tense with **depuis** is also a past tense, as in English:

> **je l'ai terminé depuis deux heures**, *I finished it two hours ago*

▶ See also **depuis** + imperfect, p. 21.

☐ **Voilà ... que, il y a ... que**

All that has been said above about **depuis** also holds good for the constructions **voilà ... que** and **il y a ... que** (*since/for*):

> **voilà (il y a) deux jours que je suis ici**, *I've been here for two days*
>
> **voilà (il y a) deux jours que je ne l'ai pas vu**, *I haven't seen him for two days (it's two days since I've seen him)*

■ Present tense with **venir de**

With **venir de** (*to have just* done something) we find a present tense of **venir** corresponding to a perfect in English:

> **je viens de déjeuner**, *I've just had lunch*

The literal sense of the French is 'I'm coming from having lunch' (present) rather than the English 'I have just had lunch' (perfect). This French construction ('I'm coming from') is a quite logical equivalent to **je vais déjeuner**, *I'm going to* have lunch (see p. 24).

▶ See also **venir de** + imperfect, p. 21.

The perfect tense

The perfect has two main uses in French; as a 'true' perfect and as a past narrative tense.

■ The 'true' perfect (≐ *I have done*)

As in English, the true perfect is used to speak of something that happened in the past and has some bearing on what is being talked about in the present:

> **j'ai mangé tous tes chocolats**, *I've eaten all your chocolates* (now there's going to be trouble!)
>
> **je suis déjà tombé trois fois**, *I've fallen over three times already* (and he's asking me to go on the ice again!)

It also corresponds to the English perfect continuous:

> **j'ai regardé la télévision tout l'après-midi**, *I've been watching television all afternoon*

Don't be tempted to use an imperfect for this—**je regardais la télévision** means *I was watching television* (when all at once something happened).

■ The past-action perfect (= *I did*)

In French, the perfect is also used for an action in past narrative, especially in speech, where English uses a simple past tense:

> **je me suis levé à sept heures, j'ai allumé la radio et je suis entré dans la salle de bains**, *I got up at seven o'clock, switched on the radio and went into the bathroom*

However, for repeated past actions, where the English simple past, *I went*, really means *I used to go* or *I would go*, French uses the imperfect:

> **on allait chaque année à Torremolinos. C'était affreux!**, *we went (= used to go) to Torremolinos every year. It was (= used to be) dreadful!*

▶ See general uses of the imperfect, below.

The imperfect tense

General uses of the imperfect

■ To indicate a repeated action:

> **il venait me chercher tous les matins à huit heures**, *he came and picked me up (used to come and pick me up; would come and pick me up) every morning at eight*

■ To indicate a continuing action (which is often then interrupted by a single action, for which the perfect or past historic is used):

> **j'épluchais des pommes de terre quand elle sonna à la porte**, *I was peeling potatoes when she rang the doorbell*

■ To indicate a continuing state of affairs:

> **j'ai regardé par la fenêtre. Il pleuvait**, *I looked out of the window. It was raining*

Imperfect or not? Choosing the right French past tense

In general, an English 'was ... ing' indicates an imperfect, and so does 'would ...', unless this has an 'if' involved or implied (*I wouldn't do that ... if I were you*), in which case the tense is the conditional—see p. 26. However, if a simple past tense is to be translated into French, you must consider whether this is one single action (past historic or perfect) or a repeated action (imperfect).

Special uses of the imperfect

■ Imperfect for a single action

More and more frequently the imperfect is used by modern writers at all levels (literature, magazines, newspapers) as a single-action tense to give greater immediacy to an event. Here the newspaper *Le Figaro* is recounting individual events—in the imperfect:

> **Côté cinéma, Bernard Borderie décidait de saisir la balle au bond. Il choisissait pour interpréter le rôle la toute jeune Michèle Mercier.** *For the film, Bernard Borderie decided to grab his opportunity. He chose a really young actress to play the part, Michèle Mercier.*

Clearly 'deciding' and 'choosing' were single, not continous or repeated, actions. The feeling behind these imperfect tenses seems to be: 'there he was, deciding, choosing ...' Though this use of the imperfect should be recognized, it is not recommended that it be imitated.

■ Imperfect with **depuis** (*for*), **depuis que** (*since*), **voilà ... que** (*since/for*) and **il y avait ... que** (*since/for*)

Where English uses a pluperfect continuous (*I had been doing*) with these expressions, French uses an imperfect:

> **j'y étais depuis deux jours**, *I had been there (for) two days*
>
> **je le voyais beaucoup plus souvent depuis que sa femme était partie**, *I had been seeing him a lot more since his wife had gone*
>
> **il y avait deux jours que j'étais là**, *I had been there for two days*

All the other rules that apply to these expressions used with the present (see pp. 17, 18) also apply when they are used with the imperfect.

■ Imperfect with **venir de** (*to have just*)

Where English uses a simple past of *have just* ..., French uses an imperfect of **venir de**:

> **je venais de déjeuner**, *I had just had lunch*

▶ Compare **venir de** + present, p. 18.

■ Imperfect in **si** sentences

After **si** meaning *if*, the simple past in English always corresponds to an imperfect in French:

> **si j'avais ton numéro, je te téléphonerais**, *if I had your number I'd phone you*

Perfect or past historic are not possible after **si** meaning *if*; nor is the conditional, which you might be tempted to use because the main verb in such sentences is usually in the conditional.

However, as in English, the conditional can be used after **si** where it really means *whether*:

> **je ne savais pas s'il rappellerait**, *I didn't know if (whether) he would phone back*

▶ See also p. 26 for the conditional in **si** sentences.

The past historic tense

The past historic is mainly, though not exclusively, a written past narrative tense. In spoken French the perfect is usually used instead to recount past actions. However, the past historic can readily be heard in some French dialects and may also be used in standard spoken French where what is being narrated is clearly a self-contained story or a historical event.

Cases where the past historic is not used

■ The past historic is an alternative to the perfect as a narrative tense—it can never be substituted for the imperfect, or for the 'true' perfect (see p. 19).

■ In letter-writing and other personal writing the perfect, not the past historic, is normally used to narrate single actions in the past.

■ The present tense (known in this case as the historic present) may quite often be found with a past meaning, substituting for the past historic. The change to the present from the past historic (or vice versa, from the historic present to the past historic) is felt to lend more immediacy to a narrative at the point at which it occurs. The following example (here, historic present to past historic at the important moment) is taken from the magazine *Marie France*:

> Ensemble le soir, ils **font** la tournée des bistrots de la Butte, ce qui ne **va** pas sans dispute ni même sans coups ... A l'époque Picasso **est** un petit gars noiraud et rablé; immenses yeux noirs, larges épaules et des hanches fines ... Le coup de foudre **se produisit** sous une pluie battante: la jeune femme courait pour se mettre à l'abri, Picasso lui **barra** le passage en lui tendant un petit chat; elle **rit** et **accepta** sans plus de façon.
>
> *In the evenings they made the rounds of the Butte pubs together, not without rows, even blows. At the time Picasso was a swarthy, broad, stocky lad, with huge black eyes, big shoulders and narrow hips. Then, in a downpour of rain, came love at first sight: the girl was running for shelter, Picasso stood in her way offering her a kitten. She laughed, and accepted without more ado.*

The change to the past historic comes at **le coup de foudre se produisit**.

■ Future for past historic

The use of the future tense instead of the past historic for past narrative is a not uncommon journalistic device. See p. 25.

The future tense

Future tense and aller + infinitive

As well as the actual future tense (**je porterai** — *I shall wear*), there is a future formed with **aller**, just as in

English futurity may be expressed by 'I am going to':

> **je vais partir**, *I'm going to leave*

This is sometimes called the 'immediate future', but the ordinary future tense can also be used for immediate happenings, and **aller** + infinitive can be used for things well into the distant future:

> **le défilé aura lieu cet après-midi**, *the procession will take place this afternoon*
>
> **on va retourner à Torremolinos l'année prochaine**, *we're going to go to Torremolinos again next year*

In fact, **aller** + infinitive is used to stress present intention:

> **je vais lui téléphoner demain matin**, *I'm going to (I intend to) phone him tomorrow morning*

or the relationship of the future event to something that is happening in the present:

> **si tu ne fais pas attention, tu vas te couper le doigt**, *if you don't look out you'll cut our finger (a direct consequence of not watching what you're doing!)*

This will often involve an event not too far into the future, but this is not necessarily the case (note the Torremolinos example above).

Special uses of the future tense

■ Future after **quand, lorsque, dès que, aussitôt que, tant que, pendant que**

Clauses beginning *when* (**quand, lorsque**), *as soon as* (**aussitôt que, dès que**), *as long as* (**tant que**) or *whilst* (**pendant que**) have a present tense in English with futurity implied. In French the tense must be future:

dès que le magasin ouvrira, nous serons à votre service, *as soon as the shop opens we shall be at your service*

With these time conjunctions French follows the strict time-logic of the situation, so that in sentences such as the following a future perfect must be used:

je te dirai quand elle sera partie, *I'll tell you when she's gone* (logically, *when she will have gone*)

Note that this strict time-logic does not extend to the conjunction **si**, *if*, which takes the same non-logical tense as English:

s'il est là quand je reviendrai, *if he's there when I get back* (present tense, **est**, not the more logical future)

■ Future as a past narrative tense

The use of the future for past narrative is also becoming more common, especially in newspaper writing. The aim is to heighten the effect with a sense of 'what was destined to happen next was …' This example comes from *Le Figaro*:

Michèle **fera** tout pour échapper à cette cage dorée. Elle **finira** par quitter la France, **tentera** une nouvelle carrière aux États-Unis, **se lancera** dans la production, **se ruinera** avec une régularité métronomique pour «monter» des films qui n'**aboutiront** guère.

Michèle did everything possible to escape from this gilded cage. She ended up leaving France, tried a new career in the United States, launched herself into production, ruined herself over and over again putting on films that had little success.

An effect similar to that of the French could be obtained in English using *was to* with each verb, but it would be considerably more clumsy than the French futures are.

The conditional tenses (conditional and conditional perfect)

General uses of the conditional

■ The conditional can show future possibility (what might or might not happen if ...):

> **je ne ferais pas ça (si j'étais à ta place)**, *I shouldn't do that (if I were you)*

The 'if' clause may or may not be expressed.

■ The conditional can also show a 'future in the past'. In this use it indicates something that is to happen subsequently to some event narrated in a past tense (*would* is used for this in English):

> **elle m'a assuré qu'elle le ferait**, *she assured me she'd do it*

Conditional tenses used in si sentences

Conditional and conditional perfect tenses are very often found in sentences that include a clause beginning with **si**:

> **je serais content si elle venait**, *I'd be pleased if she came*
>
> **si elle était venue, j'aurais été tellement heureux**, *if she'd come I'd have been so happy*

The sequence is

> **si** + imperfect, + main clause conditional
> **si** + pluperfect, + main clause conditional perfect

▶ See also p. 22.

Special uses of the conditional tense

■ The conditional may express qualified possibility:

> **il serait peut-être temps de regarder votre avenir en face**, *it might perhaps be time to face your future*

■ The conditional may be used to avoid direct responsibility for the accuracy of a statement:

> **il y aurait quinze blessés**, *there are said to be (appear to be) fifteen injured*

■ The conditional may express a polite, hesitant request:

> **vous ne pourriez pas le revendre?**, *couldn't you perhaps sell it again?*

Literary tenses

One of the simple tenses, the imperfect subjunctive, and two of the compound tenses, the pluperfect subjunctive and the past anterior, are obsolescent or literary, to be recognized but not used.

The imperfect subjunctive

This is found in subjunctive clauses with a past meaning:

> **elle ne pensait pas qu'il le sût**, *she didn't think he knew it*

Everyday French would use a present subjunctive:

> **elle ne pensait pas qu'il le sache**

The pluperfect subjunctive

■ This is used where the verb has a pluperfect meaning:

> **il téléphona, bien qu'elle fût déjà partie**, *he telephoned, even though she had already left*

Here, everyday French would use a perfect subjunctive:

il téléphona, bien qu'elle soit déjà partie

■ It is also used in literary French instead of the conditional perfect:

> **Rodrigue, qui l'eût cru? ... Chimène, qui l'eût dit? ...** *Rodrigue, who would have believed it?— Chimène, who would have said it?*
>
> (Corneille: *Le Cid*)

The past anterior

This is used with a pluperfect meaning after the conjunctions **quand, lorsque, dès que, aussitôt que**, but only when the verb in the main clause is in the past historic:

> **quand elle eut fini de parler, il se leva et sortit**, *when she had finished speaking, he got up and went out*

THE IMPERATIVE

The imperative is used to give orders or instructions or to express requests.

Formation of the imperative

The imperative has three forms, which are the same as the **tu, nous**, and **vous** parts of the present tense of the verb:

> **choisis**, *choose!*
> **choisissons**, *let's choose*
> **choisissez**, *choose!*

■ First conjugation (**-er**) verbs lose the final **-s** of the **tu** form of the imperative, unless followed by **y** or **en**:

> **donne-le-moi**, *give it to me*
> **donnes-en à ton amie**, *give some to your friend*
> **va dans ta chambre!**, *go to your room!*

So do irregular verbs whose **tu** form of the present ends in **-es**:

> **ouvre la porte**, *open the door*

► For form, order and position of pronoun objects with the imperative, see p. 106.

■ In the negative the **ne** and **pas** etc. go round the verb in the usual way:

> **ne choisissez pas encore**, *don't choose yet*

■ Third-person commands (*let him/her/it/them ...*) are expressed by using **que** plus the present subjunctive:

> **qu'il le trouve lui-même**, *let him find it himself!*

Alternatives to the imperative

An imperative need not be used to express a command. There are a number of other ways of doing it.

■ Politer than the imperative is **voulez-vous (veux-tu) ...**, *will you/would you ...*, or **auriez-vous l'amabilité de ...**, *would you be so kind as to ...*:

> **voulez-vous chercher mon sac?**, *would you look for my bag?*
> **auriez-vous l'amabilité de me passer ma valise?**, *would you be so kind as to pass me my case?*

■ The imperative of **vouloir** plus the infinitive is found as an alternative to the imperative in formal language and in the ending to formal letters:

> **veuillez signer ici**, *kindly sign here*
> **Veuillez agréer, chère madame, l'expression de mes sentiments les plus distingués**, *Yours sincerely*

■ In official notices and in recipes an infinitive, or **défense de ...**, or **... interdit** may be found instead of an imperative:

> **ne pas se pencher au dehors**, *do not lean out*
> **défense de fumer**, *no smoking*
> **entrée interdite**, *no entry*

■ The future tense may also express a command, as in English:

> **vous ferez exactement ce que je vous dirai**, *you'll do exactly what I say*

REFLEXIVE VERBS

Reflexive verbs are verbs whose direct or indirect object is the same as their subject (*he scratches himself; she allows herself a chocolate*). In French they consist of a simple verb preceded by a reflexive pronoun:

> **il arrête le train**, *he stops the train*—simple verb
> **le train s'arrête**, *the train stops (itself)*—reflexive verb

■ The reflexive pronouns

Apart from **se**, they are the same as the ordinary object pronouns:

> **me**, *(to) myself*
> **te**, *(to) yourself*
> **se**, *(to) himself, (to) herself, (to) itself, (to) oneself, (to) themselves*
> **nous**, *(to) ourselves*
> **vous**, *(to) yourself, (to) yourselves*

Me, te, and **se** become **m', t',** and **s'** before a vowel or **h** 'mute'. **Te** becomes **toi** when used with the imperative (see p. 107).

The reflexive pronoun corresponding to **on** is **se**:

> **on s'y habitue**, *you get used to it*

□ The reflexive pronouns are the same whether they are

direct or indirect objects, and stand before the verb in the same way as other object pronouns.

▶ For the order of object pronouns, including reflexives, see p. 106.

☐ Reflexive pronouns in the plural—**nous, vous, se**—as well as meaning *(to) ourselves*, *(to) yourselves*, *(to) themselves*, can also mean *(to) one another* or *(to) each other*. This includes **se** when it refers to **on** with a plural meaning (*we, you, people*, etc.):

> **ils se détestent**, *they hate each other*
> **elles se téléphonent tous les soirs**, *they phone each other every evening*
> **on s'aime**, *we love one another*

If ambiguity might otherwise result, **l'un(e) l'autre / les un(e)s les autres** is added, where the reflexive is a direct object; or **l'un(e) à l'autre / les un(e)s aux autres**, where the reflexive is an indirect object:

> **nous nous sommes demandé, si ...**, *we wondered (asked ourselves) whether ...*
> **nous nous sommes demandé l'un à l'autre, si ...**, *we asked each other, whether ...*

■ Compound tenses of reflexive verbs are formed with **être**, not **avoir**.

In compound tenses the past participle of a reflexive verb agrees with a preceding direct object. Since direct object and subject are usually the same, this means that the past participle of a reflexive verb appears to agree with its subject. However, this is not always the case:

> **elle s'est lavée**, *she washed (herself)*
> **elle s'est lavé les cheveux**, *she washed her hair*

▶ See also p. 15.

■ A French reflexive verb may correspond to an English one:

> **il se gratte**, *he scratches himself*

but very often it does not:

> **elle s'assoit**, *she sits down*
> **il se lave**, *he washes*

■ Reflexive verbs are occasionally used in French where English uses a passive:

> **je m'étonne: je croyais que c'était gratuit**, *I'm surprised, I thought it was free*
> **cela ne se vend pas ici**, *it's not sold here*

▶ See p. 34 for this and other alternatives to the passive.

■ Reflexive verbs may sometimes have the sense of 'becoming':

> **je m'ennuie**, *I'm getting bored*
> **elle s'impatientait**, *she was becoming impatient*

THE PASSIVE

The passive forms of the tenses are those where the subject of the verb experiences the action rather than performs it (active: *he helped*; passive: *he was helped*).

Formation of the passive

The passive in English is formed with parts of the verb *to be* plus the past participle; in French it is formed in exactly the same way with parts of **être** plus the past participle:

> **elle est détestée**, *she is hated*
> **il était protégé par sa femme**, *he was protected by his wife*
> **la ville avait été abandonnée par ses habitants**, *the town had been abandoned by its inhabitants*

In the passive the past participle always agrees with the subject, in the same way that an adjective would.

■ In English the 'doer' of the action is indicated by *by* (as in this sentence you're reading). This is **par**, or sometimes **de**, in French. **Par** is more specific:

> **il a été tué par sa femme**, *he was killed by his wife*
>
> **elle est bien vue de tout le monde**, *she is well regarded by everyone*

However, where *by* refers to the instrument used, rather than the person doing the action, **de** is always used in French:

> **il a été tué d'un coup de revolver**, *he was killed by a revolver shot*

■ In English, the indirect object of an active verb may be made into the subject of the corresponding passive verb:

> *someone gave the book to me → I was given the book*
>
> *Paul gave the book to me → I was given the book by Paul*

This is impossible in French. *I was given the book* can be translated using **on**:

> **on m'a donné le livre** (literally, *someone has given me the book*)

However, in the second example, *I was given the book by Paul*, where the 'doer' of the action is stated, the sentence has to remain active in French:

> **Paul m'a donné le livre**

Or, if the English sentence stresses 'Paul':

> **c'est Paul qui m'a donné le livre**

Alternatives to the passive

The passive is frequently avoided in French, especially when the 'doer' of the action is not mentioned.

■ Most frequently **on** is used:

>**on l'avait abandonné**, *it had been abandoned*

■ Sometimes a reflexive verb may be used:

>**cela ne se fait pas!**, *that's not done!*
>**la porte s'ouvre**, *the door is (being) opened* (**la porte est ouverte** would mean *the door is— already—open*)

■ Or an active form may be preferred where English would use a passive:

>**ta lettre les a bouleversés**, *they've been shattered by your letter*

■ Occasionally, where the subject is a person, **se faire** is used:

>**il s'est fait renvoyer en Espagne**, *he's been sent (got himself sent) back to Spain*
>**nous nous sommes fait renvoyer**, *we've been sacked*

PARTICIPLES

The present participle

Formation of the present participle

The present participle (in English, the *-ing* part of the verb) is formed in French by substituting **-ant** for **-ons** in the **nous** form of the present tense of the verb:

>**choisir → nous choisissons → choisissant**

There are only three present participles which are exceptions to this rule:

être: étant
avoir: ayant
savoir: sachant (but **savant** where the present
participle is used as an adjective: **un phoque
savant**, *a performing seal*)

Note also the two spellings of **fatiguant/fatigant**, the
second used adjectivally:

en fatiguant la salade, *whilst dressing the salad*
une journée fatigante, *an exhausting day*

Uses of the present participle

■ As an adjective

The present participle can be used as an adjective. When
it is so used, it behaves exactly as other adjectives. So it
agrees with its noun, and qualifying adverbs precede it:

l'année suivante, *the following year*
une femme incroyablement charmante, *an
incredibly charming woman*

■ As a verb

The present participle can also be used verbally in a
phrase with or without **en** (= *in, by, whilst*). When the
present participle is used verbally, pronoun objects stand
in front of it and adverbs after it, just as with any other
part of the verb:

**en la rencontrant un jour dans la rue, il lui a
adressé la parole**, *(on) meeting her one day in
the street, he spoke to her*

Negatives go round it, as they go round other parts of
the verb:

**ne sachant pas que vous étiez là, elle se tourna
vers moi,** *not knowing you were there, she
turned to me*

In this verbal use the present participle, since it is not an adjective, does not take adjective agreements.

☐ With or without **en**

When the present participle is used verbally without **en**, the two actions (that of the present participle and that of the main verb) follow one another. When the participle is used with **en** the actions go on simultaneously:

> **se retournant, elle répondit ...**, *turning round, she replied ...*
>
> **en tombant, elle a entraîné une lampe**, *in falling (as she fell), she brought down a lamp*
>
> **comment s'est-elle fait mal? — En tombant**, *how did she hurt herself? By falling (When she fell)*

En with a present participle usually corresponds to the English *on ... ing, by ... ing, in ... ing, whilst ... ing.*

☐ With **tout en**

The addition of **tout** to the above construction (**tout en ...**) draws attention to the fact that the two actions were going on together, often over a period of time. **Tout en** is usually translated as *whilst*:

> **tout en me parlant, il allumait sa pipe**, *whilst (all the time he was) speaking to me, he was lighting his pipe*

Tout en can also have the meaning of *whilst* (*on the one hand*):

> **tout en reconnaissant ce que vous avez fait, je dois vous dire que ...**, *whilst recognizing what you have done, I have to tell you that ...*

☐ With verbs of motion

English can make a verbal phrase by using a verb of motion plus a preposition (*swim away, fly off, run out*).

French has no equivalent construction and uses a variety of strategies to deal with these concepts (**partir à la nage, s'envoler**, etc.). One of these is to make the preposition into a verb and then add a present participle with **en**: **sortir en courant**, *run out*. This present-participle construction is most frequently found with **courir**.

▶ See also translation problems, p. 233.

■ As a noun

Present participles are occasionally used as nouns. They add **-e** for feminine, **-(e)s** for plural forms: **l'occupant**, *occupier*; **la passante**, *(woman) passer-by*; **des anciens combattants**, *old soldiers*.

▶ The present participle can never be used in French with an auxiliary verb, as it is in English. *I am sleeping* has to be **je dors**. See p. 16.

The perfect participle

In English, the perfect participle is formed with the present participle of *to have* plus the past participle of the verb. In French the perfect participle is formed in an exactly parallel way, using the present participle of **avoir** plus the past participle of the verb:

> **ayant dit cela, elle s'assit**, *having said that, she sat down*

Verbs that form their compound tenses with **être** also form their perfect participle with **être**:

> **étant arrivée de très bonne heure, elle acheta un journal**, *having arrived very early, she bought a newspaper*
>
> **s'étant déjà baigné, il revint sur la terrasse de la villa**, *having already had his dip, he came back on to the terrace of the villa*

As the above examples show, the use of the perfect participle in French exactly parallels its use in English.

The past participle

Formation of the past participle

Past participles of regular verbs are formed by removing the ending of the infinitive (**-er**, **-ir**, **-re**) and adding **-é**, **-i**, **-u**:

> **porter → porté**, *carried*
> **choisir → choisi**, *chosen*
> **vendre → vendu**, *sold*

▶ For the past participles of irregular verbs see the verb list, p. 242.

Uses of the past participle

■ The past participle is used to form all the compound tenses.

▶ See p. 3 (compound tense formation), p. 14 (past-participle agreement).

■ The past participle is used with **être** to form the passive.

▶ See p. 32.

■ The past participle may be used adjectivally; it then agrees with its noun, takes an adverb qualification, etc., just like any other adjective:

> **elle était complètement épuisée**, *she was completely exhausted*

■ The past participle may also occasionally be used as a noun:

> **le reçu**, *receipt*
> **les rescapés**, *survivors*

■ French sometimes uses a past participle where English

would use a present participle. Mostly this is to describe positions of the body. Common examples are:

accoudé, *leaning (on one's elbows)*

agenouillé, *kneeling*

appuyé, *leaning*

assis, *sitting*

couché, *lying (e.g. in bed)*

étendu, *lying (outstretched)*

(sus)pendu, *hanging*

une seule lampe était suspendue au plafond, *just one lamp was hanging from the ceiling*

il était agenouillé devant l'autel, *he was kneeling before the altar*

THE SUBJUNCTIVE

The subjunctive, expressing doubt or unreality, barely exists any longer in English (*if I were you*; *if that be so*; *would that he were*). In French, though some of its tenses are literary or archaic, it is still in constant use in both the spoken and the written language.

The subjunctive is found in subordinate clauses beginning with **que** meaning *that*, though by no means all such clauses have a subjunctive. The subjunctive in French originally showed the speaker's attitude to an event in the light of his or her emotion (doubt, disbelief, pleasure, etc.). Nowadays it has become fixed as the form used after certain verbs or certain conjunctions, most of which still express some sort of emotion. In only a limited number of cases, however, noted below, is there still a choice between using or not using the subjunctive.

Formation of the subjunctive

The subjunctive has four tenses in French. Of these only the present subjunctive and, on the not very frequent occasions where a perfect meaning is necessary, the perfect subjunctive are in modern everyday use. The tenses are formed as follows:

■ Present subjunctive

The present subjunctive is formed from the **ils** form of the present tense with endings as follows:

choisir → ils choisissent → choisiss-

je choisisse	nous choisiss**ions**
tu choisiss**es**	vous choisiss**iez**
il choisisse	ils choisiss**ent**

This normally produces, as with **choisir** above, **nous** and **vous** forms identical with those of the imperfect tense. In the few cases where this would not be so, **nous** and **vous** forms of the imperfect tense are used for present subjunctive **nous** and **vous**:

prendre → ils prennent → prenn-

je prenne	**nous prenions**
tu prennes	**vous preniez**
il prenne	ils prennent

The following verbs do not follow this pattern:

aller, avoir, être, faire, falloir, pouvoir, savoir, valoir, vouloir

▶ For the subjunctive forms of these verbs, see the list of irregular verbs, p. 242.

■ Perfect subjunctive

Use the present subjunctive of **avoir** or **être** with the past participle of the verb:

j'aie choisi	**nous ayons** choisi
tu aies choisi	**vous ayez** choisi
il ait choisi	**ils aient** choisi
je sois arrivé(e)	**nous soyons** arrivé(e)s
tu sois arrivé(e)	**vous soyez** arrivé(e)(s)
il soit arrivé	**ils soient** arrivés

■ Imperfect subjunctive

The imperfect subjunctive is based on the past historic tense, as follows:

-er verbs (past historic: **je portai**):

je port**asse**	nous port**assions**
tu port**asses**	vous port**assiez**
il port**ât**	ils port**assent** ·

-ir and **-re** verbs (past historic: **je choisis, je vendis**):

je vend**isse**	nous vend**issions**
tu vend**isses**	vous vend**issiez**
il vend**ît**	ils vend**issent**

Irregular verbs that form their past historic with **-us** etc. form their imperfect subjunctive with **-usse**:

être:	je **fusse**	nous **fussions**
	tu **fusses**	vous **fussiez**
	il **fût**	ils **fussent**

▶ See the irregular verb list, p. 242.

■ Pluperfect subjunctive

Formed from the imperfect subjunctive of **avoir** or **être** plus the past participle:

J'eusse choisi, etc.
je fusse parti, etc.

■ Future subjunctive

This tense does not exist. To express future meanings in subjunctive clauses, **devoir** must be used. See p. 67.

Uses of the subjunctive

■ The subjunctive is used after certain verbs; the ones listed are those most frequently met:

☐ Verbs of expectancy, wishing, wanting

> **vouloir que**, *wish; want*
> **souhaiter que**, *wish*
> **attendre que**, *wait until*
> **désirer que**, *want*
> **préférer que**, *prefer*
> **aimer mieux que**, *prefer*
> **il est préférable que**, *it is preferable*
> **il vaut mieux que**, *it is better*
> **il est important que**, *it is important*
>
> **il est important que tu le saches**, *it's important that you know*

With verbs of wishing, preferring, etc., English very often uses an infinitive dependent on an object—*they prefer us to go*. This is impossible in French and must always be translated by a dependent clause (= *they prefer that we should go*):

> **ils préfèrent que nous partions**, *they prefer us to go*
> **que voulez-vous qu'on fasse pour les jeunes chômeurs?**, *what do you want us to do for the young unemployed?*

Note that **espérer que**, *hope*, does not take the subjunctive.

☐ Verbs of necessity

> **il faut que**, *must*
> **il est nécessaire/urgent que**, *it is necessary/ urgent*
>
> **il faut que vous vous débrouilliez tout seul**, *you must sort it out on your own*

☐ Verbs of ordering, forbidding, allowing

> **ordonner que**, *order*
> **dire que**, *tell*

défendre que, forbid
permettre que, allow
s'opposer à ce que, be opposed (to someone
doing …)

je ne permets pas que vous voyagiez seule, I shall
not allow you to travel alone

With **dire que** there is a difference in meaning according
to whether the subjunctive is used or not:

dites au messager qu'il part ce soir, tell the courier
he's leaving tonight (piece of information)
dites au messager qu'il parte ce soir, tell the
courier to leave tonight (command)

☐ Verbs of possibility

il est possible que, it is possible
il se peut que, it is possible
il semble que, it seems
il paraît que, it seems
il est peu probable que, it is improbable
il est impossible que, it is impossible

se peut-il qu'elle soit déjà là?, is it possible that
she's there already?

Note that **il est probable que**, it is probable, and **il me
semble / me paraît que**, it seems to me, do not generally
take the subjunctive.

☐ Verbs of surprise and incomprehension

s'étonner que, be surprised
être surpris / étonné que, be surprised
quelle chance que, what luck
il me paraît curieux / surprenant / incroyable etc.
que, it seems odd / surprising / unbelievable

je m'étonne qu'il y ait autant de chômeurs, I'm
surprised there are so many unemployed

☐ Verbs of uncertainty

> **il n'est pas certain que**, *it is not certain*
> **il n'est pas évident/vrai que**, *it is not obvious/true*
> **je ne nie pas que**, *I don't deny*
> **mettons/supposons que**, *let us assume*
>
> **mettons que les réponses de ce sondage soient
> exactes**, *let us assume that the replies to this
> poll are correct*

☐ Verbs of doubt and disbelief

> **douter que**, *doubt*
> **il est douteux que**,
>   *it is doubtful*

> **penser que**, *think*
> **croire que**, *believe*
> **trouver**, *think*   in the
> **s'attendre à ce que**, *expect*   negative or
> **être sûr/certain**,   interrogative
>   *be sure/certain*

> **je ne crois pas qu'elle t'ait dit des choses pareilles**,
>   *I don't believe she said things like that to you*

With the last five verbs above there is a difference in
meaning according to whether the subjunctive is used or
not:

> **je ne pense pas qu'il pleut**, *I don't think it's raining*
>   (I'm fairly sure it isn't)
> **je ne pense pas qu'il pleuve**, *I don't <u>think</u> it's
>   raining* (though it may be)

☐ Verbs of liking, pleasure, dislike, displeasure

> **aimer que**, *like*
> **adorer que**, *love*
> **ça me plaît que**, *I'm glad*
> **être content/heureux/enchanté que**, *be glad/
>   happy/delighted*
> **détester que**, *hate*

> **j'aime que vous chantiez comme ça**, *I like you to sing like that*

☐ Verbs of regret and concern

> **regretter que**, *be sorry*
> **être désolé que**, *be sorry*
> **c'est dommage que**, *it's a pity*
> **avoir peur que ... (ne)**, *be afraid*
> **craindre que ... (ne)**, *be afraid*, (and the related conjunctions **de peur que ... (ne)**, **de crainte que ... (ne)**, *for fear that*)
> **être fâché que**, *be annoyed that*
> **avoir honte que**, *be ashamed that*
>
> **je suis désolé qu'elle ne puisse pas venir**, *I'm sorry she can't come*

▶ The use of **ne** with **avoir peur que**, **craindre que**, and **de peur/crainte que** is formal or literary. See p. 162.

■ The subjunctive is used after certain conjunctions. The common ones are:

☐ **bien que / quoique**, *although*

> **bien que tout le monde se connaisse au village, personne ne lui parlait**, *although everyone knew each other in the village, no-one would speak to him*

☐ **afin que / pour que**, *so that; for*

> **ils ont tout fait pour qu'il vienne le plus souvent possible**, *they did everything so (that) he would come as often as possible*

☐ **à moins que ... (ne)**, *unless*

> **il y aura une catastrophe à moins que vous ne trouviez une solution rapidement**, *there'll be a disaster unless you find a solution quickly*

▶ The use of **ne** (without **pas**, and with no negative

meaning) is still quite commonly found after **à moins que,** although even here it is tending to disappear except in formal or literary language. See p. 163.

☐ **que,** *whether;* **que ... que,** *whether ... whether;* **soit que ... soit que,** *whether ... whether* (literary)

> **les Français aiment le rock, qu'il soit hard ou qu'il ne le soit pas,** *the French like rock, whether it's hard or not*
>
> **qu'on parte ou non,** *whether we leave or not*

☐ **jusqu'à ce que / en attendant que,** *until*

> **restez là jusqu'à ce qu'elle vienne,** *wait there until she comes*

☐ **avant que ... (ne),** *before*

> **ne bougez pas avant qu'elle parte,** *don't move before she goes*

The subjunctive is nowadays very commonly also used after **après que,** *after,* though not in careful or literary French.

▶ The use of **ne** after **avant que** is formal or literary. See p. 163.

☐ **pourvu que / à condition que,** *provided that*

> **oui, pourvu que vous le disiez au patron,** *yes, provided that you tell the boss*

☐ **si ... que,** *however;* **qui que,** *whoever;* **quoi que,** *whatever*

> **cet édifice, si imposant qu'il soit,** *this building, however impressive it may be*
>
> **qui qu'elle soit, quoi qu'elle dise, ne la crois pas,** *whoever she is, whatever she says, don't believe her*

▶ See also p. 233.

☐ **sans que**, *without*

> **faites-le, sans que nous en sachions rien**, *do it without us knowing anything about it*

☐ **de sorte que / de façon que / de manière que**, *so that* (= *with the inention that*)

> **on le fera, de sorte que vous puissiez voir toutes les possibilités**, *we'll do it, so that you can see all the possibilities*

Note that when these conjunctions express result, they are not followed by the subjunctive:

> **on l'a fait de sorte qu'ils ont pu voir toutes les possibilités**, *we did it in such a way that they could see all the possibilities*

■ The subjunctive is also used in the following cases:

☐ To relate back to a superlative, or to the adjectives **premier, dernier, seul, unique**, which convey a superlative idea

> **la Bretagne est la première province française qu'on ait dotée d'un programme d'action,** *Britanny is the first French province to have been provided with an action programme*

The subjunctive is not always found in these constructions.

☐ To express a 'required characteristic'

> **il cherchait quelque chose qui puisse le protéger,** *he was looking for something that could protect him*

With this construction the subjunctive is not used if the thing characterized is actually known to exist:

>   **il cherchait la seule chose qui pouvait le protéger:
>   son casque**, *he was looking for the only thing
>   that could protect him, his helmet*

☐ To express a third person command

>   **que le ciel soit loué!**, *heaven be praised!*

☐ In a second 'if' clause, where **que** is substituted for **si**

>   **si tu veux nous accompagner, et que tu puisses
>   être prêt avant huit heures, on t'emmènera**, *if
>   you want to go with us, and you can be ready by
>   eight o'clock, we'll take you*

The substitution of **que** for the second **si** is not
obligatory; a second **si** would not be followed by the
subjunctive.

☐ Instead of a conditional perfect in literary French.
The tense used is the pluperfect subjunctive

>   **il ne l'eût pas fait**, *he would not have done it*

Avoiding the subjunctive

Though the French use the subjunctive a great deal in
everyday conversation, it is most frequently found after
expressions of desire, necessity, and regret (**je veux que
...**, **il faut que ...**, **je suis désolé que ...**). Otherwise it
tends to indicate high style, and expressions involving it
are avoided wherever possible. So

>   **il est possible qu'elle vienne aujourd'hui**, *it's
>   possible that she'll come today*

becomes

>   **peut-être qu'elle va venir aujourd'hui**, *perhaps
>   she'll come today*

and

> **on le fera demain, à moins qu'elle ne vienne**
> **aujourd'hui**, *we'll do it tomorrow, unless she*
> *comes today*

becomes

> **on le fera demain, si elle ne vient pas aujourd'hui**,
> *we'll do it tomorrow, if she doesn't come today*

and

> **donne-le-lui avant qu'elle parte**, *give it to her*
> *before she goes*

becomes

> **donne-le-lui avant son départ**, *give it to her before*
> *her departure*

■ The subjunctive is also avoided where both verbs would have the same subject, by using the appropriate preposition and a dependent infinitive. English frequently does this too:

> **je suis désolé d'apprendre la mauvaise nouvelle**
> **de cette façon**, *I'm sorry to hear (that I should*
> *hear) the bad news in this way* (instead of '**je**
> **suis désolé que j'apprenne la mauvaise**
> **nouvelle de cette façon**')

▶ See p. 51 for the infinitive after verbs and pp. 51, 52 for the infinitive after adjectives.

■ In the same way, the subjunctive can be avoided with impersonal verbs by using a dependent infinitive:

> **il a fallu que je repense tout → il a fallu tout**
> **repenser**, *I had to rethink everything*

If there is any ambiguity about what the subject of the infinitive is, then a subjunctive clause must be used. The use of an indirect object with the main verb (**il m'a fallu tout repenser**) is literary.

THE INFINITIVE

The infinitive, what it is

Infinitives of French regular verbs end in **-er**, **-ir**, or **-re**, corresponding to the English *to ...* form of the verb:

> **porter**, *to wear*
> **choisir**, *to choose*
> **vendre**, *to sell*

The infinitive is the 'name' of the verb: it is really a sort of noun, and as such can be the subject or object of a verb, or stand after a preposition:

> **fumer, c'est dangereux**, *smoking is dangerous*
> **défense de fumer**, *no smoking*

Notice, in the examples above, that English usually uses the *-ing* form of the verb rather than the infinitive as the verbal noun.

Some infinitives have become true nouns and take an article. They are always masculine:

> **à prendre après manger**, *to be taken after meals* (**manger**, *to eat*)
> **un homme de savoir**, *a man of learning* (**savoir**, *to know*)

■ Pronoun objects stand in front of the infinitive:

> **pour le regarder**, *in order to look at it*

■ Both parts of a negative stand in front of the infinitive and its object pronouns:

> **un film à ne pas manquer**, *a film not to be missed*
> **pour ne plus le regarder**, *in order not to look at it any more*

The infinitive after a verb

Infinitives usually follow another verb, and in English they are joined to it by *to*. In French they are joined to it by **à**, **de**, or nothing at all. Which of these is used depends on the head verb, not on the infinitive, and it doesn't vary—it is always, for instance, **se mettre à** + infinitive (*begin to*), **essayer de** + infinitive (*try to*), **vouloir** + infinitive (*want to*).

▶ For the correct preposition to use with any verb (**à**, **de**, or nothing) see the alphabetical list on pp. 59–64.

■ It is normally impossible in French for an infinitive to depend on the object of another verb as it can in English:

> *I want Fred to listen to me*—Fred is the object of *want*, but Fred is also the subject of *listen*.

A subordinate clause has to be used for this in French (see p. 42):

> **je veux que Fred m'écoute**, *I want Fred to listen to me*

However, with a verb of perceiving (seeing, hearing, feeling, etc.) a construction similar to the English one is possible:

> **je l'ai regardé travailler**, *I watched him work*

▶ See also p. 232.

The infinitive after adjectives, nouns, and adverbs

Infinitives may also follow adjectives, nouns, and adverbial expressions of quantity (**beaucoup**, **trop**, etc.).

A preposition is used before the infinitive and in most cases this is **de**:

> **je suis étonné de te voir**, *I'm surprised to see you*
> **je n'ai pas le temps de te parler**, *I haven't the time to speak to you*

Sometimes, however, the infinitive has a passive sense (*to be done* rather than *to do*), and in this case **à** is used:

> **j'ai beaucoup à faire**, *I've a lot to do* (= to be done)
> **j'ai deux pièces à tapisser**, *I've two rooms to paper* (= to be papered)
> **c'est une pièce très difficile à tapisser**, *it's a very difficult room to paper* (= to be papered).
> Compare: **il est très difficile de tapisser cette pièce**, *it's very difficult to paper this room*

There are one or two exceptions to this. In spite of the following infinitive having an active sense, **à** is always used with:

> **disposé à**, *willing to*
> **lent à**, *slow to*
> **prêt à**, *ready to*
> **prompt à**, *prompt in*
>
> **vous êtes prêts à partir?**, *you're ready to go?*

and with **unique**, **seul**, **dernier** and the ordinal numbers:

> **il était le seul à venir**, *he was the only one to come*

The infinitive after prepositions

▶ For infinitives following **à** and **de**:
after verbs, see pp. 55 and 56;
after adjectives, nouns and adverbs, see p. 51.

Infinitives may also follow the prepositions **après**, **par**, **sans**, and **pour**, and many compound prepositions formed with **de** (**au lieu de**, **avant de**, etc.):

> **sans bouger**, *without moving*
> **pour sortir**, *in order to go out*
> **je commence par citer Molière**, *I shall begin by quoting Molière*

■ In English, the part of the verb which follows a preposition is in almost all cases the present participle (*without looking*, *after eating*). In French it is always an infinitive, except after **en** where the present participle is used: **en revenant**, *on coming back*. See p. 35.

■ Always after **après**, and sometimes, according to meaning, after other prepositions, a perfect infinitive is used:

> **après l'avoir mangé**, *after eating (having eaten) it*
> **il est en prison pour avoir volé une voiture**, *he's in prison for having stolen a car*

▶ For the perfect infinitive, see below.

Other uses of the infinitive

■ In literary French the infinitive may be found, preceded by **de**, instead of a past historic:

> **et Yves de répondre «Mais non»**, *and Yves replied 'Of course not'*

■ The infinitive may also be used as an imperative. See p. 29.

The perfect infinitive

The perfect infinitive is formed with the infinitive of **avoir** or **être** plus the past participle of the verb:

>**avoir porté**, *to have worn*
>**être parti**, *to have gone*
>**s'être dépêché**, *to have hurried*

Past participles make the same agreements as in the compound tenses of the verb.

As well as being used after **après** and other prepositions (see p. 53), the perfect infinitive is used after a number of verbs where logic demands it. Common ones are:

>**se souvenir de/se rappeler**, *remember*
>**remercier de**, *thank for*
>**regretter de/être désolé de**, *be sorry for*
>**pardonner (à quelqu'un) de**, *forgive (somebody) for*

Beware: the tense of the equivalent English verb may not be the logical one!

>**je me souviens de l'avoir dit**, *I remember saying (having said) it*
>**je vous remercie d'avoir téléphoné**, *thank you for phoning (having phoned)*
>**elle est désolée de nous avoir dérangés**, *she's sorry to have (for having) disturbed us*
>**pardonne-moi de t'avoir retardé**, *forgive me for holding you up (having held you up)*

PREPOSITIONS AFTER VERBS

Prepositions with infinitives

In English a verb is linked to a following infinitive either by *to* (*I hope to go*) or by nothing at all (*I must go*). The constructions are invariable, we always use *hope + to*, *must* + *nothing*, whatever the infinitive that follows. The same is true of French, except that in French there are three possibilities, **de**, **à**, and nothing.

■ Verb + **de** + infinitive:

> **il essaye de le faire**, *he tries to do it*

This is by far the largest group and if a verb does not belong to one of the two other groups below, it should be assumed to take **de**.

■ Verb + nothing + infinitive

This is a relatively small group of rather common verbs. It includes:

☐ Verbs of expectancy (wanting, hoping)

> **j'espère vous revoir**, *I hope to see you again*

☐ Verbs of perception (seeing, hearing, feeling)

> **l'entends-tu venir?**, *can you hear him coming?*

☐ Verbs of liking and dislike

> **je déteste nager dans l'eau froide**, *I hate swimming in cold water*

☐ The modal verbs (**vouloir, pouvoir**, etc. See p. 64)

> **je ne sais pas nager**, *I can't swim*

☐ Intransitive verbs of motion (**aller, monter, sortir**, etc.)

> **va chercher ton père**, *go and look for your father* (note that the *and* used in English with these verbs is not used in French)

Pour may also be used with these verbs to stress the purpose of the action:

> **Il est entré dans le garage pour chercher une pelle**, *he went into the garage (in order) to look for a spade*

The most frequently met verbs taking an infinitive without a preposition are:

adorer, *adore*
aimer (mieux), *prefer*
aller, *go*
compter, *expect*
croire, *think*
descendre, *come down*
désirer, *want*
détester, *hate*
devoir, *have to*
écouter, *listen to*
entendre, *hear*
entrer, *come in*

envoyer, *send*
espérer, *hope*
faillir, *almost (do)*
faire, *have (done)*
falloir, *must*
laisser, *let*
monter, *go up*
oser, *dare*
paraître, *seem*
partir, *go off*
pouvoir, *can*
préférer, *prefer*

prétendre, *claim*
se rappeler, *remember*
regarder, *look at*
rentrer, *come in*
sembler, *seem*
(se) sentir, *feel*
sortir, *go out*
souhaiter, *wish*
valoir mieux, *be better*
venir, *come*
voir, *see*
vouloir, *want*

▶ For a fuller treatment of **faire** and **laisser** + infinitive see p. 71.

■ Verb + **à** + infinitive

This is also a small group of verbs. They are less heavily used, but still common. The **à** indicates aim or direction. The most frequently met verbs in this group are:

aider à, *help*
s'amuser à, *enjoy oneself*
apprendre à, *learn*
s'apprêter à, *get ready*
arriver à, *manage*
s'attendre à, *expect*
avoir à, *have*

chercher à, *try*
commencer à, *begin*
consentir à, *consent*
consister à, *consist (in)*
continuer à, *continue*
se décider à, *decide; make up one's mind*

demander à, *ask*
encourager à, *encourage*
enseigner à, *teach*
forcer à, *force*
s'habituer à, *get used*
hésiter à, *hesitate*
s'intéresser à, *be interested*
inviter à, *invite*

se mettre à, start	**perdre du temps à**, waste time	**renoncer à**, *give up*
		rester à, *be left*
obliger à, *force*	**persister à**, persist	**réussir à**, *manage*
parvenir à, *manage*		**servir à**, *be used*
passer du temps à, spend time	**pousser à**, *urge*	**songer à**, *think*
	(se) préparer à, prepare	**tarder à**, *be late*
penser à, *think*		**tenir à**, *be keen*

▶ See p. 59 for an alphabetical list of infinitive and noun constructions after verbs.

Prepositions with nouns and pronouns

Most French verbs have the same preposition before a following noun as their English equivalents. There are three main groups where this is not the case.

■ Verbs with a direct object where we should expect a preposition:

>**attendez-moi!**, *wait for me!*

The most frequently met verbs of this kind are:

approuver, *approve of*	**habiter**, *live at*
attendre, *wait for*	**mettre**, *put on*
chercher, *look for*	**payer**, *pay for*
demander, *ask for*	**regarder**, *look at*
écouter, *listen to*	**reprocher**, *blame for*
essayer, *try on*	

■ Verbs taking **de** where we should expect nothing:

>**elle joue du violon**, *she plays the violin*

The most frequently met verbs in this group are:

s'apercevoir de, *notice*	**discuter de**, *discuss*
s'approcher de, approach	**douter de**, *doubt*
	se douter de, suspect
avoir besoin de, *need*	
changer de, *change*	**s'emparer de**, *grab*

jouer de, *play*   **se méfier de**, *mistrust*
  (*an instrument*)   **se servir de**, *use*
jouir de, *enjoy*   **se souvenir de**, *remember*
manquer de, *lack*   **se tromper de**, *mistake*

■ Verbs taking **à** where we should expect nothing:

elle joue au tennis, *she plays tennis*

The most frequently encountered verbs of this kind
are:

assister à, *attend*	**renoncer à**, *renounce*
convenir à, *suit*	**répondre à**, *answer*
se fier à, *trust*	**résister à**, *resist*
jouer à, *play* (*a game*)	**ressembler à**, *resemble*
nuire à, *harm*	**succéder à**, *succeed*
(dés)obéir à, (*dis*)*obey*	(*someone*)
pardonner à, *forgive*	**survivre à**, *outlive*
(dé)plaire à, (*dis*)*please*	**téléphoner à**, *telephone*

Also in this group are a number of verbs that take **à**
with the noun at the same time as an infinitive with **de**:

j'ai dit à Jean-Pierre de ne pas sortir, *I told Jean-
Pierre not to go out*

These verbs are:

commander à ... de, *order*	**ordonner à ... de**, *order*
conseiller à ... de, *advise*	**permettre à ... de**, *allow*
défendre à ... de, *forbid*	**promettre à ... de**, *promise*
demander à ... de, *ask*	**proposer à ... de**, *suggest*
dire à ... de, *tell*	

■ Verbs taking **à** or **de** where English has an entirely
different preposition:

je l'ai acheté au fermier, *I bought it from the farmer*

These verbs are:

acheter à, *buy from*
arracher à, *snatch from*
blâmer de, *blame for*
boire à, *drink from*
cacher à, *hide from*
croire à, *believe in*
demander à, *ask for … from*
dépendre de, *depend on*
doter de, *equip with*
emprunter à, *borrow from*
enlever à, *take away from*
féliciter de, *congratulate on*
s'intéresser à, *be interested in*

louer de, *praise for*
manquer à, *be missed by*
penser à, *think about*
prendre à, *take from*
punir de, *punish for*
récompenser de, *reward for*
réfléchir à, *think about*
remercier de, *thank for*
rêver à, *dream about*
rire de, *laugh at*
servir à, *be used for*
songer à, *think about*
témoigner de, *bear witness to*
toucher à, *meddle with*
vivre de, *live on*
voler à, *steal from*

Alphabetical list of verb constructions with prepositions

The list includes both verbs + preposition + infinitive, and verbs + preposition + noun. Only 'problem' verbs are included. If a verb is not included, assume that:

■ with a noun it will take the same construction as in English

■ before an infinitive it will take **de**

Abbreviations used:

> qn—**quelqu'un**
> qch—**quelque chose**
> sb—somebody
> sth—something
> INF—infinitive

acheter à qn	*buy from sb*
adorer + INF	*adore to*
aider à + INF	*help to*
aimer + INF	*like to*
aimer mieux + INF	*prefer to*
aller + INF	*go and; be going to*
s'amuser à + INF	*have fun ... ing*
s'apercevoir de qch	*notice sth*
apprendre qch à qn	*teach sb sth*
apprendre à qn à + INF	*teach sb to*
apprendre à + INF	*learn to*
s'apprêter à + INF	*prepare to*
s'approcher de qn	*approach sb*
arracher à qn	*snatch from sb*
arriver à + INF	*manage to*
assister à qch	*attend/witness sth*
attendre qn	*wait for sb*
s'attendre à + INF	*expect to*
avoir qch à + INF	*have sth to*
avoir besoin de + INF	*need to*
blâmer de qch	*blame for sth*
boire à qch	*drink from/to sth*
cacher à qn	*hide from sb*
changer de qch	*change sth*
chercher qch	*look for sth*
chercher à + INF	*try to*
commander à qn de + INF	*order sb to*
commencer à (sometimes **de**) + INF	*begin to*

compter + INF	*intend to*
conseiller à qn de + INF	*advise sb to*
consentir à + INF	*agree to*
consentir à qch	*agree to sth*
consister en/dans qch	*consist of sth*
consister à + INF	*consist in*
continuer à (sometimes **de**) + INF	*continue to*
convenir à qn	*suit sb*
croire qn	*believe sb*
croire à/en qn/qch	*believe in sb/sth; trust in sb/sth*
se décider à + INF	*decide to; make up your mind to*
défendre à qn de + INF	*forbid sb to*
demander qn/qch	*ask for sb/sth*
demander qch à qn	*ask sb for sth*
demander à + INF	*ask to*
demander à qn de + INF	*ask sb to*
dépendre de qn/qch	*depend on sb/sth*
déplaire à qn	*displease sb*
descendre + INF	*go down and*
désirer + INF	*want to*
désobéir à qn	*disobey sb*
détester + INF	*hate to; detest … ing*
devoir + INF	*have to*
dire à qn de + INF	*tell sb to*
discuter de qch	*discuss sth*
doter de qch	*equip with sth*
douter de qch	*doubt sth*
se douter de qch	*suspect sth*
écouter qn/qch	*listen to sb/sth*
écouter qn + INF	*listen to sb … ing*
s'emparer de qch	*grab sth*
emprunter à qn	*borrow from sb*
encourager à + INF	*encourage to*

enlever à qn	*take away from sb*
enseigner qch à qn	*teach sb sth*
entendre qn + INF	*hear sb ... ing*
entrer + INF	*go/come in and*
envoyer qn + INF	*send sb to*
espérer + INF	*hope to*
essayer qch	*try sth on*
se fâcher de qch	*be annoyed about sth*
se fâcher contre qn	*be annoyed with sb*
faillir + INF	*almost do sth*
falloir + INF (**il faut**, etc.)	*must*
féliciter qn de qch	*congratulate sb on sth*
se fier à qn	*trust sb*
forcer à + INF	*force to*
habiter + PLACE	*live at/in*
habituer qn à + INF	*get sb used to ... ing*
s'habituer à + INF	*get used to ... ing*
hésiter à + INF	*hesitate to*
s'intéresser à qn/qch	*be interested in sb/sth*
s'intéresser à + INF	*be interested in ... ing*
inviter qn à + INF	*invite sb to*
jouer à qch	*play (a game)*
jouer de qch	*play (an instrument)*
jouir de qch	*enjoy sth*
laisser + INF	*let*
louer de qch	*praise for sth*
manquer de qch	*lack sth*
manquer à qn	*be missed by sb*
se marier avec qn	*marry sb*
se méfier de qn	*mistrust sb*
mettre qch	*put sth on*
se mettre à + INF	*begin to*
monter + INF	*go up (stairs) and*
nuire à qch	*harm sth*
obéir à qn	*obey sb*
obliger qn à + INF	*force sb to*

ordonner à qn de + INF	*order sb to*
oser + INF	*dare to*
paraître + INF	*appear to*
pardonner qch à qn	*forgive sb for sth*
partir + INF	*go off and; go off to*
parvenir à + INF	*manage to*
passer du temps à + INF	*spend time ... ing*
payer qch	*pay for sth*
penser à qn/qch	*think about sb/sth*
penser à + INF	*think of ... ing*
perdre du temps à + INF	*waste time ... ing*
permettre à qn de + INF	*allow sb to*
persister à + INF	*persist in ... ing*
plaire à qn	*please sb*
pousser à + INF	*urge to*
pouvoir + INF	*be able to*
préférer + INF	*prefer to*
prendre à qn	*take from sb*
préparer qn à + INF	*prepare sb to*
se préparer à	*get ready to*
prétendre + INF	*claim to*
promettre à qn de + INF	*promise sb to*
proposer à qn de + INF	*suggest to sb that they should*
punir de qch	*punish for sth*
se rappeler + PERFECT INF	*remember ... ing*
(*sometimes* **de** + PERF INF)	
récompenser de qch	*reward for sth*
réfléchir à qch	*think about sth*
regarder qn/qch	*look at sb/sth*
regarder qn + INF	*watch sb ... ing*
remercier de qch	*thank for sth*
renoncer à qch	*give sth up*
renoncer à + INF	*give up ... ing*
rentrer + INF	*come (back) in to*
répondre à qn/qch	*answer sb/sth*
reprocher qch à qn	*blame sb for sth*

résister à qch	*resist sth*
ressembler à qn/qch	*be like sb/sth*
rester à + INF	*remain to*
réussir à + INF	*manage to*
rêver à qn/qch	*dream about sb/sth*
rire de qn/qch	*laugh at sb/sth*
sembler + INF	*seem to*
sentir qch + INF	*feel sth ... ing*
se sentir + INF	*feel oneself ... ing*
servir à qch	*be used for sth*
servir à + INF	*be used to*
se servir de qch	*use sth*
songer à qn/qch	*think about sb/sth*
songer à + INF	*think about ... ing*
sortir + INF	*go out and*
souhaiter + INF	*want to*
se souvenir de qn/qch	*remember sb/sth*
succéder à qn	*succeed sb*
survivre à qn	*outlive sb*
tarder à + INF	*delay ... ing*
téléphoner à qn	*telephone sb*
témoigner de qch	*bear witness to sth*
tenir à + INF	*be keen to*
toucher à qch	*meddle with sth*
se tromper de qch	*mistake sth; be wrong about sth*
valoir mieux + INF	*be better to*
venir + INF	*come and; come to*
vivre de qch	*live on sth*
voir qn + INF	*see sb ... ing*
voler à qn	*steal from sb*
vouloir + INF	*want to*

MODAL VERBS

The modal verbs (auxiliary verbs of 'mood' like *can*, *must*, *will*, in English) always have a dependent infinitive:

je veux parler, *I want to speak*

Even if this infinitive is occasionally not expressed, it is always implied: **je veux bien!**, for instance, is really **je veux bien faire ce que tu as proposé!**

In French the five modal verbs are:

> **devoir**, *must*
> **falloir (il faut)**, *have to*
> **pouvoir**, *be allowed to*
> **savoir**, *can*
> **vouloir**, *will*

The meanings given above are in fact not really adequate. These verbs have a number of different meanings and shades of meaning in different uses of their various tenses. These are explained below.

Devoir

In its basic meaning **devoir** implies obligation, inner conviction, moral necessity (compare **falloir**, below). Its English equivalent is *have to* or *must*:

> **je dois rentrer**, *I must (have to) go home*

■ Present

As well as *have to*, **devoir** in the present tense also has the sense of *should, is supposed to, is probably ... ing*:

> **il doit être là**, *he should be there (by now)*

It can also mean *am to*:

> **je dois aller à Paris demain**, *I'm to go to Paris tomorrow*

■ Imperfect

As well as *used to have to*, the imperfect of **devoir** can also mean *was to, was due to*:

> **on devait faire la vaisselle tous les matins avant
> sept heures**, *we used to have to wash up every
> morning before seven o'clock*
> **dans trois jours la guerre devait éclater**, *in three
> days war was to break out*

■ Perfect

The basic meaning of the perfect is *had to* (or *has had to*);
the perfect also means *must have*:

> **j'ai dû prendre le train**, *I had to (I've had to) take
> the train*
> **il a dû partir plus tôt**, *he must have left earlier*

■ Pluperfect

The pluperfect meaning is *had had to*, or *must have* (*must
have* is the same as the perfect—English has no separate
pluperfect form of *must*):

> **comme la voiture était en panne, j'avais dû
> prendre le train**, *as the car was off the road, I'd
> had to take the train*
> **elle nous répondit qu'il avait dû partir plus tôt**, *she
> replied that he must have left earlier*

■ Conditional

The conditional means *would have to*, and also *ought to* or
should:

> **s'il devenait président, on devrait quitter le pays**, *if
> he became president we should have to leave
> the country*
> **cela devrait faire votre affaire**, *that ought to
> (should) do the job for you*

■ Conditional perfect

The conditional perfect means *would have had to*, and
also *ought to have* or *should have*:

s'il était devenu président, on aurait dû quitter le
  pays, *if he had become president we should
  have had to leave the country*
il aurait dû répondre, *he ought to have (should
  have) replied*

■ Present subjunctive

Verbs have no future subjunctive. The present
subjunctive of **devoir** is used where it is necessary to
give other verbs in the subjunctive a future meaning:

je suis désolé qu'elle doive te suivre par avion,
  I'm sorry she's going to fly out after you (qu'elle
  te suive *could mean she's already set out*)

■ Note that **devoir** can be used impersonally, in all
tenses, as an extension of **il y a**:

il doit y avoir trois cents personnes, *there must be
  three hundred people*

■ Used without a dependent infinitive, **devoir** means *to
owe*. In this sense it is not a modal verb:

je vous dois mille francs, *I owe you a thousand
  francs*

Falloir

The basic meaning of **falloir** is *must* or *have to*, implying
external necessity or constraint. Compare **devoir**, above.

tu dois rentrer déjà? — Mais oui, il faut
  absolument que je rentre: sinon, ma mère ne me
  permettra pas de sortir demain, *you must go
  home already? — Yes, I've really got to or my
  mother won't let me come out tomorrow*

■ **Falloir** is always an impersonal verb, used only in the
il form (**il faut**, **il fallait**, etc.). The person need not be
expressed at all if it is obvious who is involved:

> **Pierre, il faut téléphoner à ta grand–mère**, *you must phone your grandmother, Pierre*

The real subject can be expressed by a dative:

> **il me faut partir**, *I have to go*

but this is rather formal, and spoken French prefers a subjunctive clause if it is necessary to say who is involved:

> **il faut que je parte**, *I've got to go*

Pouvoir

Pouvoir means basically *can* or *be allowed to*. Parts of the English verb *can* are missing and *be able to* or *be allowed to* has sometimes to be substituted when translating.

> **peut-on sortir par ici?**, *can we (are we allowed to) go out this way?*
> **l'eau est bonne, on pourra nager**, *the water's fine, we'll be able to go swimming*

As well as *be allowed to* and *can*, **pouvoir** can also mean *may*, either as the politer form of *can*, or expressing possibility:

> **puis-je parler à votre patron?**, *may I speak to your boss?*
> **il peut toujours venir**, *he may still come*

Note too the reflexive form, **se pouvoir**:

> **cela se peut**, *that's possible*

■ Perfect

Means *was able to* or *could* (in a past sense), or *may have*:

> **je n'ai pas pu ouvrir la boîte**, *I couldn't open the tin*

> **elle a pu se tromper de train**, *she may have got the wrong train*

■ Conditional

Means *would be able to* or *could* (in a conditional sense), and also *might*:

> **si tu payais, je pourrais t'accompagner**, *if you paid I could (would be able to) come with you*
> **je crois qu'il pourrait neiger**, *I think it might snow*

■ Conditional perfect

Means *would have been able to* or *could have*, also *might have*:

> **si tu avais payé, j'aurais pu t'accompagner**, *if you'd paid, I could have (would have been able to) come with you*
> **elle aurait pu se présenter avant le début du spectacle**, *she might have turned up before the play started*

■ **Pouvoir** can be used impersonally as an extension of **il y a**:

> **il pourrait y en avoir mille**, *there might be a thousand of them*

■ With verbs of perception (**entendre, voir, sentir**) English uses *can* or *could* where French prefers the simple verb:

> **je le voyais atterrir**, *I could see it landing*

Savoir

Savoir means *can* in the sense of *know how to*. Compare **pouvoir** above.

> **l'eau est bonne, on peut nager — Mais moi, je ne sais pas nager**, *the water's fine, we can go swimming—But I can't swim*

■ Conditional

In careful or formal language, the negative conditional of **savoir** is used as a politer form of *I can't*. In this use the **pas** is always omitted:

> **je ne saurais faire cela**, *I don't really think I can do that*

With the full negative **je ne saurais pas** means *would not know how to, couldn't* (in a moral sense):

> **je ne saurais pas faire quelque chose comme ça**, *I couldn't do anything like that*

■ **Savoir** is most frequently found used without a dependent infinitive, meaning *to know*. In this use it is not a modal verb:

> **je sais qu'elle est là**, *I know she's there*

Vouloir

The basic meaning of **vouloir** is *to wish* or *want*:

> **je veux vous dire quelque chose**, *I want to tell you something*

It also means *will, be willing to*. **Bien** is used where English stresses *will*:

> **oui, je veux bien le faire**, *yes, I will do it*
> **la moto ne veut pas démarrer**, *the bike won't start*

It can also mean *attempt to* or *intend to*:

> **j'ai voulu l'embrasser**, *I tried to kiss her*
> **qu'est-ce qu'il veut faire?**, *what does he mean to do?*

■ Conditional, conditional perfect

As well as *should wish*, *should want* (conditional), and *should have wished*, *should have wanted* (conditional perfect), these tenses also have the meanings *should like* and *should have liked*:

> **je voudrais être à sa place**, *I'd like to be in her place*
>
> **j'aurais voulu la revoir**, *I'd have liked to see her again*

With this meaning **je voudrais** is a standard way of asking politely for things:

> **je voudrais deux cents grammes de pâté s'il vous plaît**, *I'd like two hundred grams of pâté, please*

■ Vouloir may also be used as a polite form of the imperative.

► See p. 29.

FAIRE + INFINITIVE AND SIMILAR CONSTRUCTIONS

Faire + infinitive

Faire + infinitive means *to have something done, to get something done, to get someone to do something*:

> **j'ai fait téléphoner à ses parents**, *I've got someone to phone his parents*
>
> **elle a fait enlever ce qui restait du repas**, *she had what was left of the meal taken away*

■ Position of objects with **faire** + infinitive

☐ Noun objects of either verb follow both verbs

> **tu as fait jouer Pierre?**, *you got Pierre to play?*
>
> **tu as fait repeindre la porte?**, *you've had the door painted?*

☐ Pronoun objects of either verb come before both verbs

> **tu l'as fait jouer?**, *you got him to play?*
> **tu l'as fait repeindre?**, *you've had it painted?*

☐ If both verbs need an object, the object of **faire** is indirect (**à ...**), since in French a double direct object is impossible.

> **la nouvelle a fait perdre son sang-froid à mon
> père**, *the news made my father lose his temper*

■ **Faire** + reflexive verbs

If the dependent verb is reflexive it loses its object pronoun:

> **je les ai fait asseoir** (not **s'asseoir**), *I got them to
> sit down*
> **elle les a fait taire**, *she shut them up*

So if you find a reflexive pronoun in this construction it must belong to **faire** (*have oneself ..., get oneself ...*):

> **elle s'est fait virer du lycée**, *she got herself thrown
> out of school*

■ Agreement of past participle of **faire**

In the **faire** + infinitive construction the past participle **fait** is invariable: it never agrees with a preceding direct object. See the last two examples above (**je les ai fait ..., elle s'est fait ...**).

Laisser, voir, entendre, sentir + infinitive

■ **Laisser** + infinitive means *to let something be done* or *to let someone do something*:

> **tu l'as déjà laissé revenir?**, *you've let him come
> back already?*

j'ai dû le laisser passer, *I had to let him go through*

■ **Voir/entendre/sentir** + infinitive mean *to see/hear/ feel something happen*:

on l'a vu partir, *we saw him go*
je me sens guérir, *I can feel myself getting better*

■ All points made above with regard to **faire** concerning objects and past participle agreement may also apply to this group of verbs, though they are quite often ignored:

tu lui as laissé repeindre ta porte?, or very often
tu l'as laissé repeindre ta porte?, *you've let him paint your door?*

English equivalents of faire, etc. + infinitive

Some infinitive constructions of the verbs considered above are the equivalent of a simple verb or a verb plus preposition in English. The most common are:

entendre dire que, *hear that*
entendre parler de, *hear about*
faire entrer, *let in; show in*
faire sortir, *let out; show out*
faire venir, *send for*
faire voir, *show*
laisser tomber, *drop*

Similar constructions with other verbs used with an infinitive are:

aller chercher, *go for*
envoyer chercher, *send for*
venir chercher, *come for*
vouloir dire, *mean*

IMPERSONAL VERBS

Impersonal verbs are verbs whose subject is **il** or **ce/cela** meaning *it* or *there*.

Impersonal verbs with il

These are of two kinds: those that are always constructed with **il**, and those where **il** is simply a temporary subject so that the real subject can be held back until later in the sentence.

■ Real subject **il**

In this group are:

☐ Weather verbs, e.g.

> **il pleut**, *it's raining*
> **il neige**, *it's snowing*
> **il gèle**, *it's freezing*
> **il tonne**, *it's thundering*
> **il y a du brouillard**, *it's foggy*
> **il fait du vent**, *it's windy*
> **il fait beau**, *it's fine*
> **il fait mauvais**, *the weather's bad*
> **il fait chaud/froid**, *it's hot/cold*

☐ **Être** used with time of day

> **il est cinq heures**, *it's five o'clock*
> **il est midi et demi**, *it's half past twelve*
> **il est tard**, *it's late*

☐ **Il y a**, *there is, there are*

> **il y a trente mille personnes dans le stade**, *there are thirty thousand people in the stadium*

Il y a is always singular.

▶ **Il y a** can also be used with **devoir** and **pouvoir**: **il peut y avoir ...**, *there may be ...* See pp. 67 and 69.

☐ A large number of other impersonal expressions, of which some of the commonest are:

>**Il s'agit de**, *it's a question of; it's about*
>**Il m'est arrivé de**, *I happened to*
>**Il faut (que)**, *you (we, they, etc.) must/need*
>**Il paraît que**, *it appears that*
>**Il semble que**, *it seems that*
>**Il suffit de**, *you only have to*
>**Il vaut mieux**, *it's better to*

Notice also

>**Il était une fois**, *once upon a time*

■ **Il** to hold back the real subject

Any verb can be used in this way; it remains singular, agreeing with **il**, even if the real subject is plural:

>**Il pousse beaucoup de fleurs au Sahara**, *there are lots of flowers (that grow) in the Sahara*
>**Il reste encore dix minutes**, *there are ten minutes still left*
>**Il me manque dix francs**, *I need ten francs* (literally: *there is lacking to me ten francs*)

☐ The real subject may be a noun, as in the examples above; or it may be a clause

>**Il me brûlait les lèvres de demander à quoi ça servait**, *I was dying to ask what that was for*

☐ The real subject may be an infinitive clause, following an adjective plus **de**. The pattern is: **il est** + adjective + **de** + infinitive clause

>**Il est difficile de concevoir quelque chose de plus imposant**, *it is difficult to conceive of anything more impressive*

In spoken French **c'est** is often used instead of **il est** in this construction.

□ The real subject may be a clause introduced by **que**, following an adjective. The pattern is: **il est** + adjective + **que** + clause

> **il est évident qu'elle mange trop**, *it's obvious that she eats too much*

Here too, **c'est** is often used instead of **il est** in spoken French.

Impersonal verbs with ce or cela/ça as subject

Ce (*it*) is used as the subject of **être**, and **cela/ça** (*it, that*) as the subject of any verb (including **être**), to stand for a previously expressed clause:

> **il est facile de mentir — Ah oui, c'est facile**, *it's easy to tell lies—Oh yes, it's easy* (**c'** refers back to **de mentir**)
>
> **si elle ment, c'est qu'elle ne veut pas vous parler de Jean-Claude**, *if she's lying, it's because she doesn't want to talk to you about Jean-Claude* (**c'** refers back to **si elle ment**)
>
> **tout ce que j'ai dit me paraît évident — Oui, cela prouve que tu es fou**, *everything I've said seems obvious to me—Yes, that proves you're crazy!* (**cela** refers back to **tout ce que j'ai dit me paraît évident**)

C'est + adjective is also used extremely often in spoken French instead of **il est** + adjective:

> **c'est** (for: **il est**) **facile de mentir — Ah oui, c'est facile**

Articles

Articles are words like *a* and *the*. Nouns are rarely used without an article in French. If the noun has no article in English, it is most likely to have a definite article in French. There are, however, quite a number of exceptions to this—see below.

THE DEFINITE ARTICLE

The definite article (*the* in English) has four forms, **le**, **la**, or **l'** with singular nouns, **les** with plural nouns. **Le** is used before a masculine singular noun, **la** before a feminine singular noun, **l'** before a singular noun of either gender beginning with a vowel or **h** 'mute'*. **Les** is used before a plural noun of either gender:

> **le garçon**, *the boy*; **la fille**, *the girl*; **le haricot**, *the bean*
>
> **l'homme**, *the man*; **l'arbre**, *the tree*
>
> **les garçons**, *the boys*; **les filles**, *the girls*; **les haricots**, *the beans*;
>
> **les hommes**, *the men*; **les arbres**, *the trees*

Le and **les** compound with **à** and **de** to produce **au**, **aux** (*to the*) and **du**, **des** (*of the*), thus:

---

* In older French some **h**'s were pronounced and some were not, which accounts for **le haricot** and **l'homme**. There is no pronunciation difference in modern French (no **h**'s are pronounced), and there are no rules to decide whether an **h** is 'mute' or not.

$$à + le = au \qquad de + le = du$$
$$à + les = aux \qquad de + les = des$$

A la and à l', de la and de l' do not change.

The same changes are found in the compound words **auquel, auxquels, auxquelles** (*to whom; to which*) and **duquel, desquels, desquelles** (*of whom; of which*).

Using the definite article

The definite article is used in French in a number of places where we should omit it in English.

■ When generalizing:

> **aimez-vous les animaux?**, *do you like animals?*
> (i.e. animals in general)

■ With abstract nouns:

> **c'est comme ça, la vie**, *life's like that*
> **l'amour de la patrie**, *love of country*

But not with abstract nouns after **avec** and **sans**:

> **avec difficulté**, *with difficulty*
> **sans occupation**, *unemployed*

■ With parts of the body, especially when used as the object of a verb:

> **levez le bras**, *raise your arm*

A reflexive indirect object pronoun is added in this construction when the action is done to, rather than with, the part of the body mentioned:

> **elle s'est lavé le visage**, *she has washed her face*

■ With names preceded by adjective or titles:

> **le vieux Corneille**, *old Corneille*
> **le président Mitterrand**, *President Mitterrand*

■ With names of countries, areas, mountains, lakes:

> **l'Angleterre**, *England*; **la Corse**, *Corsica* (but **en Angleterre**, **d'Angleterre**, *in/from England*; **en Corse**, **de Corse**, *in/from Corsica*); **le Mont-Blanc**, *Mont Blanc*; **le lac Trasimène**, *Lake Trasimeno*

■ With names of languages:

> **j'apprends le français**, *I'm learning French* **tu parles bien le français**, *you speak French well*

The article is omitted, however, after **parler** where the name of the language follows without any other qualification:

> **il parle français**, *he speaks French*

■ With days, mealtimes, seasons, religious festivals:

> **je déteste le lundi**, *I hate Monday(s)* **tu prends le petit déjeuner?**, *do you want breakfast?* **c'est l'hiver qui revient**, *winter's back* **le vendredi saint**, *Good Friday* **la Toussaint**, *All Saints' Day* (but the article is omitted with **Pâques**, *Easter*, and **Noël**, *Christmas*)

■ With school subjects and games:

> **aimes-tu les maths?**, *do you like maths?* **ici, on joue au rugby**, *here they play rugby* **il déteste les sports**, *he hates games*

Definite article for indefinite article

The definite article is used in a number of places where we should use the indefinite article (*a, an*).

■ When expressing quantity after price:

> **douze francs le kilo**, *twelve francs a kilo*
> **cent francs la bouteille**, *a hundred francs a bottle*

■ When expressing speed:

> **cent vingt kilomètres à l'heure**, *120 km an hour*
> (note the addition of **à** in French)

■ French also uses a definite article in a number of set expressions where in English we should use an indefinite article or no article at all:

> **il s'est couché le dernier/le premier**, *he went to bed last/first*
> **l'un d'eux**, *one of them*
> **au lit**, *in bed*
> **au régime**, *on a diet*
> **à la maison**, *at home*
> **à l'école**, *at school*
> **à l'église**, *in church*

Omission of the definite article

The definite article is omitted in French in forming an attributive noun (a noun used as an adjective):

> **du pâté de campagne**, *country pâté*
> **un tronc d'arbre**, *a tree trunk*
> **les fromages de France**, *French cheeses*

Compare these with:

> **un goût de la campagne**, *a taste of the countryside*
> **le tronc de l'arbre**, *the trunk of the tree*
> **le nord de la France**, *the north of France*

THE INDEFINITE AND PARTITIVE ARTICLES

It is convenient to consider these two forms of article together, since there is much similarity in their use in French.

The indefinite article, what it is

The indefinite article (*a*, *an*, *some/any* in English) has three forms: **un** with masculine singular nouns, **une** with feminine singular nouns, **des** with plural nouns:

> **un garçon**, *a boy*; **une fille**, *a girl*; **un haricot**, *a bean*
> **un homme**, *a man*; **un arbre**, *a tree*
> **des garçons**, *some boys*; **des arbres**, *some trees*

The partitive article, what it is

The partitive article (*some* in English, or *any* in questions and after negatives) has three forms, **du**, **de la**, and **de l'**. They are used before singular 'uncountable' nouns, i.e. nouns like *milk*, *sugar*, etc. that cannot normally be used in the plural. **Du** is used before a masculine noun, **de la** before a feminine noun, **de l'** before a noun of either gender beginning with a vowel or **h** 'mute':

> **du chocolat**, *some chocolate*
> **de la confiture**, *some jam*
> **de l'argent**, *some money*

The partitive is sometimes said to have a plural form, **des**. Strictly speaking, however, **des** is the plural of the indefinite article: the singular of **des vins** is **un vin**, not **du vin**.

Du/de la/des or le/la/les?

English sometimes does not use any article at all before nouns:

> **vous prenez du lait?**, *do you take milk?*
> **je déteste le lait**, *I hate milk*

This raises the problem of whether to use **du/de la/des** or **le/la/les** where English has a noun with no article. **Du/de la/des** particularizes, **le/la/les** generalizes: **du/de la/des** means 'some', **le/la/les** implies 'all'. So:

> **vous avez du jus d'orange?**, *do you have orange juice?* (i.e., some orange juice)
>
> **j'aime le jus d'orange**, *I like orange juice* (i.e., orange juice in general, all orange juice)
>
> **il y a des mouches dans ma soupe**, *there are flies in my soup* (some flies, not all the flies that exist)
>
> **je n'aime pas les mouches**, *I don't like flies* (all flies, any flies at all, not just some flies)

De for des, etc.

■ After a negative the indefinite article (**un/une/des**) and the partitive article (**du/de la/de l'**) become **de** (**d'** before a vowel or **h** 'mute'). English may use *any* for this:

> **j'ai du temps**, *I have time*
>
> **je n'ai pas de temps à perdre**, *I've no time (I haven't any time) to lose*
>
> **il n'y a pas de pellicule dans l'appareil-photo**, *there isn't any film in the camera*
>
> **je n'ai pas d'appareil-photo**, *I don't have (haven't got) a camera*

Ne ... que is not regarded as negative as far as this rule is concerned:

> **je n'ai qu'un très vieil appareil**, *I've only a very old camera*

A negative *is* followed by an indefinite or partitive article if what is negated is the identity of the noun:

> **ce n'est pas un train, c'est un tramway**, *it isn't a train, it's a tram*

■ The plural indefinite article **des** becomes **de** (**d'** before a vowel or **h** 'mute') when the noun following is preceded by an adjective:

> **j'ai eu d'incroyables difficultés**, *I've had unbelievable difficulties*

This rule is often ignored where the meaning of the phrase centres on the noun rather than the adjective:

> **des jolies filles**, *pretty girls*

It is always ignored where the adjective + noun pair forms a set expression:

> **des petits pois**, *peas*
> **des petits pains**, *bread rolls*

Before the adjective **autres**, however, you must keep to **d'**:

> **d'autres voyageurs ont dit ...**, *other travellers have said ...*

■ After the preposition **de** (*of*) the partitive article **du/ de la/de l'** and the plural indefinite article **des** are always omitted:

> **j'ai besoin d'argent**, *I need (some) money*
> **c'était un grand cratère plein d'eau**, *it was a great crater full of (some) water*

This means that expressions of quantity, which all incorporate the preposition **de** (*of*), omit **du/de la/de l'/ des**:

> **un verre de vin**, *a glass of wine*
> **beaucoup de vin**, *a lot of wine*

But note that the definite article, meaning *the*, is NOT omitted in such cases:

j'ai acheté une bouteille du vin qu'il nous a fait goûter, *I bought a bottle of the wine he let us taste*

Nor is the indefinite article in the singular omitted:

il lui restait quelques bouteilles d'un vin très ancien, *he still had a few bottles of a very old wine*

The expressions of quantity **encore** (*more*) and **bien** (*many*) are intensifying adverbs not incorporating the preposition **de** and are followed by **du/de la/des**:

encore du pain, s'il vous plaît!, *more bread please!*

bien des gens disent cela, *many people say that*

Omission of the indefinite article

The indefinite article is omitted in French in the following cases where, in the singular, it would be used in English.

■ In apposition (i.e., where a second noun is placed directly after a first one in order to explain it):

M. Duval, ancien combattant de la guerre de quatorze-dix-huit, *M. Duval, a veteran of the 14–18 war*

Definite articles, however, are not dropped in apposition:

M. Duval, l'ancien combattant dont nous parlons, *M. Duval, the veteran we're speaking about*

■ After **il est/elle est**/NOUN **est**, followed by the name of a profession:

il est menuisier, *he's a joiner*

son fils est avocat, *his son's a lawyer*

But not after **c'est**:

> **c'est un menuisier**, *he's a joiner*

■ After **quel!**:

> **quel imbécile!**, *what a fool!*

■ After **sans**:

> **les voyageurs sans billet**, *passengers without a ticket*

The partitive article is also omitted in this case, as in English:

> **une journée sans vin est une journée sans soleil**, *a day without wine is a day without sunshine*

■ In lists, both the indefinite article and the partitive article may be omitted, as in English:

> **on y voyait des moutons**, *sheep could be seen there*

but:

> **on y voyait moutons, vaches, porcs, poules, tous mélangés**, *sheep, cattle, pigs, chickens could be seen there, all higgledy piggledy*

> **on nous offrait du mouton**, *we were offered lamb*

but:

> **on nous offrait mouton, porc, veau, bœuf ... toutes sortes de viandes**, *we were offered lamb, pork, veal, beef—all kinds of meat*

This use is rather literary.

Nouns

GENDER OF NOUNS

English has three genders: masculine, feminine, and neuter (*he*, *she*, *it*). French has only two: masculine and feminine. Most nouns denoting male people are masculine, most denoting female people are feminine. Names of inanimate objects may be either masculine or feminine. Unlike English nouns, French nouns make their gender obvious by means of the article in front of them and the adjectives that go with them.

The rules for gender in French are very far from watertight and there are many exceptions to all of them. As an overall rule of thumb for an unknown noun: if it ends in **-e** it is more likely to be feminine, if not it is more likely to be masculine.

Masculine groups

■ Workers, traders, names of males, and many names of animals are masculine:

> **le constructeur**, *builder*; **le boulanger**, *baker*; **le lion**, *lion*; **le fils**, *son*

Many but not all of these also have feminine forms: see p. 93. **Une autruche** (*ostrich*), **la baleine** (*whale*), **la girafe** (*giraffe*), **la panthère** (*panther*), **la souris** (*mouse*), **la fourmi** (*ant*) are always feminine.

■ Days, months, seasons, weights, measures, numerals, fractions, points of the compass, languages are masculine:

> **le vendredi**, *Friday*; **(le) janvier**, *January*; **le printemps**, *spring*; **le kilo**, *kilo*; **le kilomètre**, *kilometre*; **le douze**, *twelve*; **le quart**, *quarter*; **le sud**, *south*; **le français**, *French*

Exceptions: **la livre**, *pound*; **la tonne**, (*metric*) *ton*; **la moitié**, *half*

■ Trees, shrubs, metals are masculine:

> **le hêtre**, *beech*; **le laurier**, *laurel*; **le fer**, *iron*

Exceptions: **la bruyère**, *heather*; **la ronce**, *bramble*; **une aubépine**, *hawthorn*

■ Countries, rivers, vegetables and fruit not ending -e are masculine:

> **le Japon**, *Japan*; **le Nil**, *Nile*; **le chou**, *cabbage*; **le citron**, *lemon*

■ Most nouns of English origin are masculine:

> **le baby-foot**, *pin-table football*; **le hit-parade**, *hit parade*

Exception: **une interview**, *interview*

■ Words not originally nouns, when used as nouns, are masculine:

> **un joli rose**, *a pretty pink*
> **un oui suivi d'un non**, *a yes followed by a no*
> **on peut apporter son manger**, *you may bring your own food*

Exception: adjectives and participles used as nouns have the gender that their ending shows. So: **le passant, la passante**, *passer-by*; **une allée**, *path*; **la nouvelle**, *piece of news*; **la sortie**, *way out*

■ Nouns with the following endings are masculine:

-acle and **-icle**:
le **spectacle**, *show*; un **article**, *article*

-age:
le **garage**
Exceptions: la **cage**, *cage*; une **image**, *picture*;
la **nage**, *swimming*; la **page**, *page*; la **plage**,
beach; la **rage**, *rage, rabies*

-ail:
le **travail**, *work*

-asme and **-isme**:
le **sarcasme**, *sarcasm*; le **communisme**,
communism

-c:
le **lac**, *lake*

-é:
le **péché**, *sin*

-eau:
le **bateau**, *boat*
Exceptions: une **eau**, *water*; la **peau**, *skin*

-ège:
le **collège**, *secondary school*

-ème:
le **poème**, *poem*
Exception: la **crème**, *cream*

-er and **-ier**:
le **clocher**, *steeple*; le **papier**, *paper*
Exceptions: la **mer**, *sea*; la **cuiller**, *spoon* (also
spelled, and always pronounced, **cuillère**)

-ment:
le **sentiment**, *sentiment*
Exception: la **jument**, *mare*

-oir:
le **couloir**, *corridor*

-ou:
le **trou**, *hole*

■ Concrete nouns ending **-eur** are masculine:

> **le moteur**, *engine*

Abstract nouns ending **-eur** are feminine: **la grandeur**, *greatness*

■ Common traps! The following nouns ending **-e** look extremely feminine—they are all masculine:

> **le crime**, *crime*; **le disque**, *record*; **le groupe**, *group*; **le manque**, *lack*; **le mélange**, *mixture*; **le reste**, *remainder*; **le risque**, *risk*; **le silence**, *silence*; **le vice**, *vice*

Feminine groups

■ Feminine forms of traders, workers, animals; names of females:

> **la boulangère**, *baker*; **une électricienne**, *electrician*; **la lionne**, *lioness*; **la fille**, *girl*

Many feminine forms, for historical reasons, do not exist; many others (like **l'électricienne** above) are being newly coined; some (e.g. **la mairesse**, *mayoress*, i.e., *mayor's wife*) can still only refer to the wife of the male. In the animals group, no feminine forms exist of **un éléphant**, *elephant*, **un hippopotame**, *hippopotamus*, **le vautour**, *vulture*.

▶ See also p. 93 for the formation of feminine nouns.

■ Countries, rivers, vegetables and fruit ending **-e** are feminine:

> **la Hollande**, *Holland*; **la Tamise**, *Thames*; **la poire**, *pear*; **la carotte**, *carrot*; **la marguerite**, *daisy*

Exceptions: **le Mexique**, *Mexico*; **le Danube**; **le Rhône**; **le légume**, *vegetable*

■ Shops and trades, arts and sciences, religious festivals are feminine:

> **la boucherie**, *butcher's*; **la menuiserie**, *joinery*; **la sculpture**, *sculpture*; **la chimie**, *chemistry*; **la Pentecôte**, *Whitsun*; **la Toussaint**, *All Saints' Day*

Exception: **un joyeux Noël**, *happy Christmas* (but, in some parts of France, **à la Noël**, short for **à la fête** (*festival*) **de Noël**)

■ Nouns with the following endings are feminine:

> **-ace**:
>> **la grâce**, *grace*
>> Exception: **un espace**, *space*
>
> **-ade**:
>> **la baignade**, *bathing*
>> Exceptions: **le grade**, *grade*; **le stade**, *stadium*
>
> **-ance** (and the similarly pronounced endings
> **-anse, -ence, ense**):
>> **la dépendance**, *dependence*; **la danse**, *dance*; **la conscience**, *conscience*; **la défense**, *defence*
>> Exception: **le silence**, *silence*
>
> **-che**:
>> **la tâche**, *task*
>> Exceptions: **le manche**, *handle*; **le reproche**, *reproach*; **le caniche**, *poodle*
>
> **-ée**:
>> **la matinée**, *morning*
>> Exceptions: **le musée**, *museum*; **le lycée**, *sixth-form college*
>
> **-elle**:
>> **la querelle**, *quarrel*
>
> **-ère**:
>> **la lumière**, *light*
>> Exceptions: **le frère**, *brother*; **le père**, *father*; **le cimetière**, *cemetery*; **le mystère**, *mystery*; **le caractère**, *character*; **le cratère**, *crater*

-esse:
>   **la faiblesse**, *weakness*

-ie:
>   **la pluie**, *rain*
>
>   Exceptions: **le génie**, *genius*; **un incendie**, *fire*;
>   **le parapluie**, *umbrella*

-ine and **-une**:
>   **la piscine**, *swimming pool*; **la fortune**, *fortune*

-ion:
>   **la concentration**, *concentration*
>
>   Exceptions: **le camion**, *lorry*; **un espion**, *spy*

-ison (and **-aison**):
>   **la prison**, *prison*; **la maison**, *house*
>
>   Exceptions: **le bison**, *bison*; **le vison**, *mink*

-oire:
>   **la foire**, *fair*
>
>   Exceptions: **le laboratoire**, *laboratory*; **le**
>   **pourboire**, *tip*; **un observatoire**,
>   *observatory*; **l'ivoire**, *ivory*

-onne:
>   **la couronne**, *crown*

-te (and **-tte**, **-ette**):
>   **la date**, *date*; **la patte**, *paw*; **la buvette**, *bar*
>
>   Exception: **le squelette**, *skeleton*

-té and **-tié**:
>   **la beauté**, *beauty*; **la pitié**, *pity*
>
>   Exceptions: **le côté**, *side*; **le comté**, *county*; **le**
>   **traité**, *treaty*; **le pâté**, (*meat, fish*) *pâté*

-ure:
>   **la nature**, *nature*
>
>   Exceptions: **le murmure**, *murmur*; **le mercure**,
>   *mercury*

Very many of the above are abstract nouns: most abstract nouns, whatever their endings, are in fact feminine.

■ Abstract nouns ending **-eur** are feminine:

>   **la chaleur**, *heat*

Exceptions: **le bonheur**, *happiness*; **le malheur**, *unhappiness*; **un honneur**, *honour*; **le déshonneur**, *dishonour*; **le labeur**, *labour*

Concrete nouns ending **-eur** are masculine: **le carburateur**, *carburettor*

■ Common traps! The following nouns ending in a consonant look extremely masculine—they are all feminine:

la chair, *flesh*; **la clef**, *key*; **la croix**, *cross*; **la façon**, *way, manner*; **la faim**, *hunger*; **la soif**, *thirst*; **la souris**, *mouse*; **la vis**, *screw*

Nouns with different meanings according to gender

masculine	*feminine*
l'aide, *assistant (male)*	**l'aide**, *assistance; assistant (female)*
le crêpe, *crêpe*	**la crêpe**, *pancake*
le critique, *critic*	**la critique**, *criticism*
le faux, *forgery*	**la faux**, *scythe*
le livre, *book*	**la livre**, *pound*
le manche, *handle*	**la manche**, *sleeve* (**la Manche**, *English Channel*)
le manœuvre, *labourer*	**la manœuvre**, *manœuvre*
le mémoire, *memorandum*	**la mémoire**, *memory*
le mode, *method; way*	**la mode**, *fashion; manner*
le mort, *dead man*	**la mort**, *death*
le moule, *mould*	**la moule**, *mussel*
un office, *office; religious service*	**une office**, *pantry*

le page, *page(boy)*	**la page**, *page (of a book)*
le pendule, *pendulum*	**la pendule**, *clock*
le physique, *physique*	**la physique**, *physics*
le poêle, *stove*	**la poêle**, *frying pan*
le poste, *set (e.g. TV); (military) post; (fire, police) station*	**la poste**, *post (= mail); post office*
le somme, *nap*	**la somme**, *sum*
le tour, *trick; tour*	**la tour**, tower
le vapeur, *steamer (boat)*	**la vapeur**, *steam*
le vase, *vase*	**la vase**, *mud; silt*
le voile, *veil*	**la voile**, *sail*

Gender of compound nouns

There are many exceptions, but

■ Compounds of two nouns or a noun plus adjective take the gender of the (first) noun:

le chou-fleur, *cauliflower*

■ Compounds where the first element is part of a verb are masculine:

le tire-bouchon, *corkscrew*

■ When in doubt about the gender of a compound noun, choose masculine.

FEMININE OF NOUNS

Professions, positions, nationalities, names of relationships, domestic animals (and a few wild ones) mostly have both masculine and feminine forms according to sex:

le vendeur, *salesman*	**la vendeuse**, *saleswoman*
le Français, *Frenchman*	**la Française**, *Frenchwoman*
le cousin, (*male*) *cousin*	**la cousine**, (*female*) *cousin*
le chien, *dog*	**la chienne**, *bitch*

With professions and positions the feminine form quite often still means *wife of the* ..., though this is not the case with the newer professions:

la mairesse, *mayoress; wife of the mayor*
l'informaticienne, (*female*) *computer programmer*

With animals, where two forms exist, the masculine form is used as the general term; the feminine form is only used where a specific distinction of sex is being made. Exception: **la chèvre** (general term for *goat*; masculine is **le bouc**, *billy-goat*)

■ The regular feminine endings are:

masculine noun	*feminine form*
-e	no change
le Russe, *Russian*	**la Russe**
-er	**-ère**
un ouvrier, *worker*	**une ouvrière**
-eur	**-euse**
le dormeur, *sleeper*	**la dormeuse**
-f	**-ve**
le veuf, *widower*	**la veuve**
-en, -on, -et	**-enne, -onne, -ette**
le chien, *dog*	**la chienne**
le Breton, *Breton*	**la Bretonne**
le cadet, *junior*	**la cadette**
-teur	**-teuse**: where the noun is based on the present participle of a verb

-trice: in all other cases

| le menteur, *lier* | la menteuse (p.p. mentant) |
| le directeur, *director* | la directrice (p.p. dirigeant) |

-x   -se

un époux, *spouse, husband*   une épouse

With other endings the feminine, where it exists, is formed by adding -e:

| un ami, *friend* | une amie |
| un Anglais, *Englishman* | une Anglaise |

■ Nouns with an irregular feminine form:

masculine	*feminine*
un abbé, *abbot*	une abbesse
un ambassadeur, *ambassador*	une ambassadrice
un âne, *donkey*	une ânesse
le canard, *drake*	la canne, *duck*
le chat, *cat*	la chatte
le comte, *count*	la comtesse
le compagnon, *companion*	la compagne
le copain, *pal*	la copine
le dieu, *god*	la déesse
le dindon, *turkey*	la dinde
le duc, *duke*	la duchesse
un empereur, *emperor*	une impératrice
le fils, *son*	la fille, *daughter*
le Grec, *Greek*	la Grecque
le héros, *hero*	l'héroïne
l'hôte, *host*	l'hôtesse
un inspecteur, *inspector*	une inspectrice
le jumeau, *twin*	la jumelle

le loup, *wolf*	la louve
le maître, *master*	la maîtresse
le mulet, *mule*	la mule
le nègre (pejorative), *negro*	la négresse
le neveu, *nephew*	la nièce
le paysan, *peasant*	la paysanne
le pécheur, *sinner*	la pécheresse
le prêtre, *priest*	la prêtresse
le prince, *prince*	la princesse
le Suisse, *Swiss*	la Suissesse
le tigre, *tiger*	la tigresse
le traître, *traitor*	la traîtresse
le Turc, *Turk*	la Turque

■ Nouns with an entirely different feminine form.

As in English, the feminine form may be expressed by an entirely different word. Among the commonest of these are:

masculine	*feminine*
le cerf, *stag*	la biche, *hind*
le cheval, *horse*	la jument, *mare*
le coq, *cock*	la poule, *hen*
l'étalon, *stallion*	la jument, *mare*
le frère, *brother*	la sœur, *sister*
le garçon, *boy*	la fille, *girl*
l'homme, *man*	la femme, *woman*
le mari, *husband*	la femme, *wife*
l'oncle, *uncle*	la tante, *aunt*
le parrain, *godfather*	la marraine, *godmother*
le père, *father*	la mère, *mother*
le porc, *pig*	la truie, *sow*
le roi, *king*	la reine, *queen*
le serviteur, *servant*	la servante, *servant*
le taureau, *bull*	la vache, *cow*

■ Nouns unchanged in the feminine form:

un/une enfant, *child*

plus masculine nouns ending **-e**.

■ Nouns with only one gender, whatever the sex of the person they refer to:

un ange, *angel*
un amateur, *lover, amateur*
un assassin, *killer*
un auteur, *author*
le cadre, *executive*
la connaissance, *aquaintance*
le député, *MP*
le docteur, *doctor*
la dupe, *dupe*
un écrivain, *writer*
le facteur, *postman*
le guide, *guide*
un imposteur, *imposter*
un ingénieur, *engineer*
le juge, *judge*

le maire, *mayor*
le médecin, *doctor*
le ministre, *minister*
le peintre, *painter*
la personne, *person*
le poète, *poet*
le possesseur, *owner*
le professeur, *(secondary) teacher*
(but, slang **le/la prof**)
la recrue, *recruit*
la sentinelle, *sentry*
le spectateur, *spectator*
le soldat, *soldier*
le témoin, *witness*
la vedette, *star*
la victime, *victim*

With professions, a specifically female form can be produced where needed by using **une femme** and adding the name of the profession attributively:

une femme auteur, *woman author, authoress*

Feminine forms of some of the above are now appearing in French (e.g., **une ministre**). They are not yet fully accepted and are at present best avoided.

For names of animals with only one gender (which is most animals), specifically male and female forms can be produced by using the adjectives **mâle, femelle**:

une souris mâle, *a male mouse*
un hamster femelle, *a female hamster*

PLURAL OF NOUNS
Plural formation

French nouns add **-s** to form their plural, except:

■ Nouns ending **-s**, **-x**, **-z** remain unchanged:

le tas, *heap*	**les tas**
la croix, *cross*	**les croix**
le nez, *nose*	**les nez**

■ Nouns ending **-au**, **-eau**, **-eu** add **-x**:

le tuyau, *drainpipe*	**les tuyaux**
le gâteau, *cake*	**les gâteaux**
le neveu, *nephew*	**les neveux**

Exceptions: **le bleu** (*bruise*) → **les bleus**; **le pneu** (*tyre*) → **les pneus**

■ Nouns ending **-al** change their ending to **-aux**:

le journal, *newspaper*	**les journaux**

Exceptions: **le bal** (*dance*) → **les bals**; **le festival** (*festival*) → **les festivals**

■ Four nouns ending **-ail** change it to **-aux** instead of adding **-s**:

le corail, *coral*	**les coraux**
l'émail, *enamel*	**les émaux**
le travail, *work*	**les travaux**
le vitrail, *stained-glass window*	**les vitraux**

■ Seven nouns ending **-ou** add **-x** instead of -s:

le bijou, *jewel*	**les bijoux**
le caillou, *pebble*	**les cailloux**
le chou, *cabbage*	**les choux**
le genou, *knee*	**les genoux**
le hibou, *owl*	**les hiboux**
le joujou, *toy*	**les joujoux**
le pou, *louse*	**les poux**

■ Letter names remain unchanged in the plural:

> **cela s'écrit avec deux p**, *you write it with two p's*

■ Family names usually remain unchanged in the plural; famous historical names add an **-s**:

> **les Robinson**, *the Robinsons*
> **les Bourbons**, *the Bourbons*

■ Irregular plurals:

l'aïeul, *ancestor*	**les aïeux**
le bonhomme, *fellow*	**les bonshommes**
le ciel, *sky*	**les cieux**
l'œil, *eye*	**les yeux**
madame, *Mrs*	**mesdames**
mademoiselle, *Miss*	**mesdemoiselles**
monsieur, *Mr*	**messieurs**

■ The following nouns have an extra meaning in the plural:

le ciseau, *chisel*	**les ciseaux**, *chisels; scissors*
la lunette, *telescope*	**les lunettes**, *telescopes; spectacles*
la vacance, *vacancy*	**les vacances**, *vacancies; holidays*
la gage, *pledge*	**les gages**, *pledges; wages*
l'affaire, *affair*	**les affaires**, *affairs; business*

Plural of compound nouns

There are many exceptions, but the following rules may help.

■ Compound nouns written as a single word, the plural is **-s**:

> **le pourboire**, *tip*   **les pourboires**

■ Compound nouns formed of an adjective plus a noun or two nouns, both add **-s**:

> **la belle-mère**, *mother-in-law*   **les belles-mères**
> **le chou-fleur**, *cauliflower*   **les choux-fleurs**

■ Compound nouns formed of a noun plus a prepositional phrase, only the noun adds **-s**:

> **un arc-en-ciel**, *rainbow*   **des arcs-en-ciel**

■ Compound nouns formed of a noun preceded by a preposition, the plural is the same as the singular:

> **le hors-d'œuvre**, *starter*   **les hors-d'œuvre**

■ Compound nouns formed of a verb plus its object noun, the noun adds **-s**:

> **le tire-bouchon**, *corkscrew*   **les tire-bouchons**
> **un essuie-glace**, *windscreen-*   **des essuie-glaces**
> *wiper*

But many compounds of this kind do not change in the plural:

> **le coupe-circuit**, *circuit-*   **les coupe-circuit**
> *breaker*

■ Compound nouns formed without a noun component, the plural is the same as the singular:

> **le passe-partout**, *master key*   **les passe-partout**

Singular for plural

■ Plural (or usually plural) in English, but singular in French are:

> **le bétail**, *cattle*; **la famille**, *family*; **la police**, *police*

The verb that follows them must be singular:

> **la famille est à table**, *the family are sitting down to a meal*

■ Singular in English, but plural in French are:

> **les funérailles**, *funeral*; **les nouvelles**, *news*; and (usually) **les fiancailles**, *engagement*; **les progrès**, *progress*

The verb that follows them must be plural:

> **les funérailles sont lundi prochain**, *the funeral is next Monday*

Pronouns

SUBJECT PRONOUNS

The subject pronouns are

singular	*plural*
je, *I*	**nous**, *we*
tu, *you*	**vous**, *you*
il, *he, it*; **elle**, *she, it*	**ils**, **elles**, *they*

Je becomes **j'** before a word beginning with a vowel or **h** 'mute'.

■ **Il** is used for a person or a thing when referring to a masculine noun, **elle** when referring to a feminine noun.

■ **Ils** (*they*) is used to refer to more than one masculine (people or things) or a mixture of masculines and feminines, **elles** (*they*) to refer to more than one feminine.

■ **Vous** can be either plural:

> **toi et ta famille, vous êtes déjà allés en Corse?**,
> *have you and your family already been to
> Corsica?*

or a formal or polite form of the singular:

> **pourriez-vous ouvrir la fenêtre, monsieur?**, *will you
> please open the window (sir)?*

The polite **vous** is always used to strangers; **tu** is
normally used to a close friend or colleague, a relation, a
fellow-student. **Tu** is always used to address a child or an
animal. Said to a stranger it may be purposely impolite.
The same applies of course to all related forms (**ton**, **le
tien**, etc.; **votre**, **le vôtre**, etc.).

■ The subject pronoun **on** takes the same form of the
verb as *il*. It means *one* in the sense of 'people in
general', and often corresponds to an indefinite *we* or *they*
in English:

> **on part à trois heures trente-six**, *we leave at 3.36*
> **on écrit des choses vraiment incroyables**, *they
> write some really unbelievable things*

In spoken French **on** is almost always used instead of
nous:

> **où on va ce soir?**, *where are we going tonight?*

On may be seen as feminine or plural when
agreements are made, but it does not have to be:

> **ton père et moi, on était si fatigué(s)**, *we were so
> tired, your father and I*

▶ **On** is frequently used in French instead of the
passive. See pp. 33, 34.

■ **Ce** (*this*, *that*, *it*, *those*) is used as an impersonal
subject pronoun, but only with the verb **être**. In the

plural **ce** is used with a plural form of **être** (**ce sont**,
c'étaient, etc.):

> **c'est une Citroën**, *it's a Citroën*
> **ce sont des mouettes**, *those are seagulls*

With verbs other than **être** (and sometimes with **être**
too), **cela** or the less formal **ça** is used:

> **ça (cela) ne se voit pas**, *that's (it's) not obvious*

▶ See also pp. 75, 76, and 225 for the use of **c'est** or **il
est** + adjective and p. 84 and p. 224 for **c'est** or **il
est** + noun.

▶ The stressed or disjunctive pronouns, **moi, toi,** etc.
may also be used as subject pronouns in some
circumstances. See p. 110.

OBJECT PRONOUNS

Forms of the object pronouns

■ The direct object pronouns are:

singular	*plural*
me, *me*	**nous,** *us*
te, *you*	**vous,** *you*
le, *him, it*; **la,** *her, it*	**les,** *them*

■ The indirect object pronouns are:

singular	*plural*
me, *to me*	**nous,** *to us*
te, *to you*	**vous,** *to you*
lui, *to him, to her, to it*	**leur,** *to them*

English often omits the *to* of the indirect object: *give it
(to) me.* If you are not clear whether an English object
without a *to* is indirect or not, simply insert the *to* and
see if the sentence still makes sense.

■ The reflexive object pronouns are the same whether direct or indirect. They are:

singular	*plural*
me, (*to*) *myself*	**nous**, (*to*) *ourselves*
te, (*to*) *yourself*	**vous**, (*to*) *yourself/ yourselves*
se, (*to*) *him-/her-/itself*	**se**, (*to*) *themselves*

► For the use of the reflexive pronouns see p. 30.

■ **Me, te, le, la, se** become **m', t', l', l', s'** before a vowel or **h** 'mute'.

Me and **te** become **moi** and **toi** in the positive imperative (**m'** and **t'** before a vowel). See p. 28 (formation of the imperative) and p. 106 (pronouns with the imperative).

■ **Y** (*to it, there*) and **en** (*of it, some*) are also treated as object pronouns. See p. 107.

Position of object pronouns

Object pronouns stand immediately before the verb (this includes infinitives, present participles, **voici** and **voilà**):

> **je t'explique le problème**, *I'll explain the problem to you*
>
> **je vais t'expliquer le problème**, *I'm going to explain the problem to you*
>
> **en t'expliquant le problème**, *by explaining the problem to you*
>
> **le voilà, le problème**, *that's it, that's the problem*

In the compound tenses they stand immediately before the auxiliary verb (**avoir** or **être**):

> **l'as-tu trouvé?**, *have you found it?*
>
> **je l'ai trouvé dans l'armoire**, *I found it in the cupboard*

Since they stand immediately before the verb, object pronouns follow the **ne** of a negative:

> **je ne l'ai pas trouvé**, *I haven't found it*

▶ For the position of object pronouns with the imperative, see below.

Order of object pronouns

Where two object pronouns appear together they stand in this order:

me, m'				
te, t'	le, l'			
se, s'	la, l'	lui		
nous	les	leur	y	en
vous				

> **je te l'apporte**, *I'll bring it to you*
> **elle le lui a emprunté**, *she's borrowed it from him*
> **il n'y en a pas**, *there isn't any*

Pronouns from the first and third columns cannot appear together. In the rare cases where this would happen the dative object is expressed by **à** + a disjunctive pronoun:

> **je vais vous conduire à eux**, *I'm going to take you to them* (not '**vous leur**')

Order of pronouns with the imperative

■ With the negative imperative the order of pronouns is as above:

> **ne me l'explique pas!**, *don't explain it to me!*

■ With the positive imperative, object pronouns follow the verb, are hyphenated to it and to each other, and stand in the following order:

	moi, m'		
	toi, t'		
le	lui		
la	nous	y	en
les	vous		
	leur		

So:

> **donne-les-lui**, *give them to him*
> **donnez-la-leur**, *give it to them*

Me and **te** become **moi** and **toi** in the positive imperative; before **en** they become **m'** and **t'** and are not followed by a hyphen:

> **donne-les-moi**, *give them to me*
> **donne-m'en**, *give me some*

The pronouns y and en

■ **Y** stands for **à, sur** or **dans** + a thing or things. In this sense it usually means *to, at, in it/them*:

> **je m'y oppose formellement**, *I'm absolutely opposed to it*
> **il ne s'y intéresse pas du tout**, *he's not in the least interested in it*

It can also mean *there*, in which case it is really an adverb, though it still behaves as an object pronoun as far as its position in the sentence is concerned:

> **on y sera à l'ombre**, *we'll be in the shade there*

■ **En** stands for **de** + a thing or things. In this sense it usually means *of, with, from it/them*:

> **nous en parlerons demain**, *we'll speak of it tomorrow*

> **trois voyageurs en sont descendus**, *three passengers got out of it*

It often means *of it*, *of them* with an expression of quantity:

> **j'en ai beaucoup**, *I've got a lot of it*
> **il y en a trois**, *there are three of them*

With expressions of quantity English frequently drops *of it/them*. This is impossible in French—the **en** must always be there:

> **il faudra en remplacer un**, *you'll have to replace one (of them)*

With expressions of quantity, **en** can also stand for **de** + persons:

> **combien de frères as-tu? — J'en ai trois**, *how many brothers have you?—I've got three*

En can also mean *some* or *any*:

> **tu en as? Alors, donne-m'en**, *have you got any? Well, give me some*

Object pronouns to complete the sense

We have an example above (**il faudra en remplacer un**) of **en** used to complete the sense in French where in English *of it/them* is often omitted. This also occurs with the pronouns **le** (= *it*) and **y**:

> **je te l'ai dit**, *I told you (so)*
> **vous êtes la fille de cet homme? — Non, je le lui ai déjà dit**, *you are this man's daughter?—No, I've already told him (it)*
> **oui, j'y vais**, *all right, I'm going (there)*
> **elle sera déjà partie, je le sais**, *she'll have gone, I know (it)*

However, with **savoir** this **le** is very often dropped in a simple response to a statement:

> **elle est là — Oui, je (le) sais,** *she's there—Yes, I know*

DISJUNCTIVE PRONOUNS

The disjunctive, or stressed, pronouns are those that stand separated from ('disjoined from') verbs. There are no separate forms for these pronouns in English, ordinary subject or object pronouns being used. In French the disjunctive pronouns are:

moi, *me*	**nous,** *us*
toi, *you*	**vous,** *you*
lui, *him*	**eux,** *them* (masculine)
elle, *her*	**elles,** *them* (feminine)

The disjunctive corresponding to **on** is **soi**. It means *oneself, yourself,* and is only used after a preposition or **que** (see below). **Soi** in fact is the disjunctive that corresponds to all the indefinite pronouns (**chacun, tout le monde, personne,** etc.). See p. 127.

Disjunctives usually only refer to people, not to things. For the corresponding usage with things, see p. 112.

Use of the disjunctive pronouns

■ Disjunctives may stand completely alone in response to a question or statement:

> **qui l'a pris? — Moi!,** *who's taken it?—Me!*
> **tu l'as pris! — Moi?,** *you've taken it!—(What) me?*

■ They are used after prepositions:

> **comme nous**, *like us*
> **la plupart d'entre elles**, *most of them*
> **c'est à moi**, *it's mine* (*it belongs to me*)
> **chacun pour soi**, *each one for himself*

■ The preposition **à** plus a disjunctive pronoun is used with certain verbs instead of an indirect object, to refer to people. These verbs are:

> **penser/songer à**, *think about*
> **avoir affaire à**, *have business with; deal with*
> **prendre garde à**, *beware of*
>
> **je pense à toi**, *I'm thinking of you*

A disjunctive after **à** is also used with **venir** and **aller** where movement in space is indicated:

> **elle est venue à moi**, *she came to me*

but not otherwise:

> **ce kilt ne te va pas du tout**, *that kilt really doesn't suit you*

■ Disjunctive pronouns are used to specify the individual parts of a plural subject. A subject pronoun may or may not appear as well:

> **eux et moi, on se voit souvent**, *they and I see each other a lot*
> **les enfants et lui se taquinent toujours**, *he and the children always tease each other*
> **qui l'a fait, lui ou son copain?**, *who did it, he or his pal?*

■ They are used to give a subject or object pronoun more emphasis:

> **moi, je ne suis pas d'accord**, *I don't agree*
> **lui, je ne l'aime pas du tout**, *I don't like **him** at all*

■ They are used after **c'est, c'était**, etc. In this sense the disjunctives may refer to things as well as people:

> **c'est toi?** *it's you?*
> **c'est eux/elles!**, *it's them!*

In careful speech or writing **ce sont eux/elles** is used.

■ They are used after **que** in comparatives and after **ne ... que**, *only*, and **ne ... ni ... ni**, *neither ... nor*:

> **elle est plus jolie que moi**, *she's prettier than me*
> **on parle toujours des choses qui n'intéressent que soi**, *we always talk about things that only interest ourselves*

■ They are used before a relative pronoun:

> **lui, qui ne sait absolument rien, a été promu capitaine**, *he, who knows absolutely nothing, has been promoted captain*
> **elle m'aime, moi qui n'ai pas un sou**, *she loves me, I who haven't a penny*

This usage is rather literary.

■ They are used instead of subject pronouns with **aussi** and **seul**:

> **lui seul est resté dans la chambre**, *he alone remained in the room*
> **eux aussi l'ont essayé**, *they tried it too*

■ They combine with **-même** to produce emphatic forms:

moi-même, *myself*	**nous-mêmes**, *ourselves*
toi-même, *yourself*	**vous-même(s)**, *yourself*; *yourselves*
lui-même, *himself*	**eux-mêmes**, *themselves*
elle-même, *herself*	**elles-mêmes**,
soi-même, *oneself* etc.	*themselves*

> **tu l'as vraiment fait toi-même?**, *you really did it
> (all by) yourself?*

Substitutes for the disjunctive pronouns

The disjunctive pronouns are not normally used to refer
to things. For a preposition + *it/them* an adverb is
substituted:

> **sur lui → dessus**, *on it*
> **dans lui → dedans**, *in it*
> **derrière lui → derrière**, *behind it*
> **après lui → après**, *after it*
> **à côté de lui → à côté**, *beside it*
> etc.
>
> **qu'est-ce qu'il y a dessus? Et dedans?**, *what's on
> it? And in it?*

Alternatively a demonstrative pronoun may be used:

> **je n'ai jamais eu une moto comme celle-là**, *I've
> never had a bike like it*

RELATIVE PRONOUNS

Relative pronouns introduce a clause within the sentence
and usually relate it back to a noun in the main clause. In
English they are *who, whom, whose, which, that, what.* In
French they are:

> **qui**, *who, which, that*
> **que**, *whom, which, that*
> **ce qui, ce que**, *what*
> **lequel**, *which*
> **de qui** or **dont**, *of whom, whose*

> **duquel** or **dont**, *of which, whose*
> **à qui**, *to whom*
> **auquel**, *to which*

and the less common

> **ce dont**, *that of which*
> **ce à quoi**, *that to which*

Que and **ce que** become **qu'** and **ce qu'** before a vowel. **Qui** and **ce qui** never change.

Relatives are sometimes omitted in English. In French this is not possible and it is important to recognize that a sentence like 'the man you want to see is here' has a hidden relative (*who* or *that*):

> **le client que tu voulais voir est là**, *the customer (that/who) you wanted to see is here*

Qui and que

■ **Qui** is the subject of the clause it introduces, **que** is the direct object:

> **la femme qui parle**, *the woman who is speaking*
> **la femme que tu connais**, *the woman (that) you know*

So **que** will be followed by a subject noun or pronoun (**tu** above), and **qui** will be followed by a verb, possibly preceded by **ne** and/or an object pronoun.

■ **Que** may not be the object of the verb it introduces but of an infinitive depending on that verb. This is similar to English:

> **la femme que tu espères épouser**, *the woman that you hope to marry* (you hope to marry her, you don't 'hope' her, so **que** is actually the object of **épouser**, not of **espères**)

■ After **que** a noun subject and the verb are often inverted if nothing else follows in that clause:

> **voilà la liste que réclame l'inspecteur**, *here's the list the inspector is asking for*

This does not happen with pronoun subjects, or if something else follows in the clause:

> **voilà la liste que vous demandez**, *here's the list you're asking for*
>
> **voilà la liste que l'inspecteur a demandée hier**, *here's the list the inspector asked for yesterday*

■ Beware! As well as being a relative, meaning *who, which, that*, **que** may also be a conjunction meaning *that* (this too may be omitted in English):

> **j'espère que tu te portes bien**, *I hope (that) you are well*

and it may also be part of a comparison, meaning *than*:

> **il est plus grand que toi**, *he's bigger than you*

Que = *what*, **qui** = *who*, and **lequel** = *which* may also introduce questions; here the question mark makes their meaning clear:

> **que dis-tu?**, *what are you saying?*

▶ See p. 118.

■ In order to avoid ambiguity **lequel** may sometimes be used instead of **qui/que**. This is because **lequel** shows gender and number:

> **j'ai écrit au père de sa femme, lequel est très riche**, *I've written to his wife's father, who is very rich*

▶ For the declension of **lequel** see p. 116.

Relative pronouns after prepositions

■ After prepositions **qui** is used for people (English *whom* or *that*). So *with/without/under whom* is **avec/sans/ sous qui**:

> **la femme avec qui je parle**, *the woman to whom I'm speaking* (*that I'm speaking to*)

Notice that in English (as in the bracketed version above) we try to avoid the old-fashioned and formal word *whom*. So we often use *that* as the relative and push the preposition to the end of the clause. This is impossible in French: the preposition must come immediately before the relative.

□ After the prepositions **parmi**, *among*, and **entre**, *between*, **lesquels/lesquelles** is used instead of **qui** for people

> **les mineurs parmi lesquels tu vis**, *the miners among whom you live*

▶ For the declension of **lequel** see p. 116.

□ **De + qui** usually becomes **dont**, *whose, of whom.*

The word order after **dont** (or **de qui** or **duquel**) is always subject, verb, rest of clause. This is not the case in English, where the object is placed immediately after the word *whose*:

> **voilà l'homme dont (de qui) tu as volé la voiture**, *there's the man whose car you stole*

English also drops the definite article (*whose car*) which French does not (**dont ... la voiture**).

Dont is used as the relative (for both people and things) with verbs that have an object preceded by **de**:

> **l'homme dont tu as besoin**, *the man you need* (= *of whom you have need*)

■ After prepositions **lequel** is used for things. So *with/without/under which* is **avec/sans/sous lequel**. **Lequel** declines as follows:

	singular	*plural*
masculine	**lequel**	**lesquels**
feminine	**laquelle**	**lesquelles**

Lequel agrees in gender and number with the noun it refers back to.

□ **Lequel** combines with the prepositions **à** and **de** to produce the forms **auquel, auxquels, à laquelle, auxquelles** and **duquel, desquels, de laquelle, desquelles**

> **les autorités auxquelles j'écris,** *the authorities I'm writing to*
>
> **le pays duquel je parle,** *the country I'm speaking about*

However, the simpler word **dont**, *of which, whose*, is often substituted for **duquel** etc.

> **le pays dont je parle,** *the country I'm speaking of*
>
> **la voiture dont il a volé la radio,** *the car whose radio he stole*

Similarly, **où**, *where*, is often used instead of **auquel, dans lequel, sur lequel**, etc. where the meaning allows it:

> **la maison où (dans laquelle) il a passé sa vie,** *the house where (in which) he spent his life*

▶ See p. 115 for the word order after **dont** and **duquel**.

■ In English *whose* can be used after a preposition: *the nurse, without whose efforts I shouldn't be here.* **Dont** cannot be used in this way in French: **de qui/duquel** must be used instead:

> **cette infirmière, sans les soins de qui je ne serais plus ici, ne travaille plus dans cet hôpital**, *that nurse, without whose efforts I should no longer be here, doesn't work in this hospital any more*

This construction is often clumsy in French, however, and is usually avoided:

> **sans les soins de cette infirmière, je ne serais plus ici; mais elle ne travaille plus dans cet hôpital**, *without that nurse's efforts I should no longer be here today; but she doesn't work in this hospital any more*

Ce qui, ce que, ce dont, ce à quoi

■ *What* as a relative is **ce qui** or **ce que**, **ce qui** being the subject form and **ce que** the object form, as with **qui** and **que**. These relative pronouns introduce noun clauses:

> **je ne comprends pas ce que tu dis**, *I don't understand what you're saying*

If the main verb following a noun clause introduced by **ce qui/ce que** is **être**, a comma and **ce** are introduced, like this:

> **ce qui est difficile, c'est de jouer de la cornemuse**, *what's difficult is playing the bagpipes*

This construction is extremely common.

■ **Ce qui** and **ce que** are used instead of **qui** and **que** as relatives after **tout**, *all*, *everything*:

> **tout ce que tu dis est incompréhensible**, *everything (that) you say is incomprehensible*

■ **Ce qui** and **ce que** can also mean *which*, where this refers to an idea rather than a specific thing:

> **il va jouer de la cornemuse, ce qui est très difficile**, *he's going to play the bagpipes, which is very difficult* (*which* refers not to bagpipes but to playing them)

After prepositions the form of the relative meaning *which*, and referring back to an idea, is **quoi**:

> **je lui ait tout expliqué, sans quoi il aurait été vraiment fâché**, *I've explained everything to him, without which he would have been really angry* (*which* refers to my having explained things to him)

■ When the verb used in the relative clause takes **à** or **de** before its object, *what* as a relative is **ce à quoi** (**à** verbs) or **ce dont** (**de** verbs):

> **ce à quoi je pense, c'est d'aller jouer à la pétanque**, *what I'm thinking of is going to play pétanque* (the verb is **penser à**)
> **je peux t'envoyer ce dont tu as besoin**, *I can send you what you need* (*what you have need of*) (the verb is **avoir besoin de**)

De quoi is sometimes used instead of **ce dont**:

> **je ne comprends pas de quoi tu parles**, *I don't understand what you're talking about*

INTERROGATIVE PRONOUNS

The interrogative pronouns in English are *who?*, *what?*, and *which?* In English they have the same forms in both direct and indirect questions:

> *who did it?*—direct question
> *I want to know who did it*—indirect question

In French they have somewhat different forms in direct and in indirect questions.

Interrogative pronouns in direct questions

Referring to people

■ As the subject of the sentence the interrogative pronoun referring to people is **qui est-ce qui** or just **qui**. Both mean *who*:

> **qui est-ce qui arrive?**, *who's coming?*
> **qui vous a dit ça?**, *who told you that?*

The interrogative pronoun **qui** is always masculine singular—even if you know that the people who turned up were feminine and plural, you still ask **qui est arrivé?**

■ As the object of the sentence the interrogative pronoun referring to people is **qui est-ce que** or just **qui**. Both mean *who* (in older or formal English, *whom*). The **que** changes to **qu'** before a vowel:

> **qui est-ce qu'on a élu?**, *who did they elect?*
> **qui as-tu envoyé?**, *who did you send?*

■ After a preposition the interrogative pronoun referring to people is **qui est-ce que** or just **qui**. Both mean *who(m)*. The **que** changes to **qu'** before a vowel:

> **pour qui avez-vous fait cela?**, *who did you do it for? (for whom did you do it?)*
> **de qui est-ce que tu parles?**, *who are you talking about? (about whom are you talking?)*

Notice that in English the preposition may (and usually does) go to the end of its clause. This is impossible in French—it must always stand before the interrogative pronoun.

■ The longer forms of the interrogatives are common in speech.

Referring to things

■ As the subject of the sentence the interrogative pronoun referring to things is **qu'est-ce qui**, *what*:

> **qu'est-ce qui arrive?**, *what's happening?*

Notice that there is no alternative form here.

■ As the object of the sentence the interrogative pronoun referring to things is **qu'est-ce que** or just **que**. Both mean *what*. In both, **que** changes to **qu'** before a vowel:

> **qu'est-ce qu'on a trouvé?**, *what did they find?*
> **qu'as-tu fait de mon pullover blanc?**, *what have you done with my white pullover?*

Notice also the form **qu'est-ce que c'est qu'un ...?** (sometimes shortened to **qu'est-ce qu'un ...?**) meaning *what's a ...?*

> **qu'est-ce c'est qu'un ornithorynque?**, *what's a duck-billed platypus?*

■ After a preposition the interrogative pronoun referring to things is **quoi**, *what*:

> **avec quoi as-tu fait cela?**, *what did you do that with? (with what did you do that?)*

■ The longer forms of the interrogatives are common in speech.

Interrogative pronouns in indirect questions

Referring to people

■ The interrogative pronoun in indirect questions referring to people is always **qui**, *who(m)*, whether it is used as subject, object or after a preposition:

> **je ne sais pas qui sera président**, *I've no idea who will be president*

je me demande qui vous allez choisir, *I wonder who you'll choose*

dis-moi à qui tu penses, *tell me who you're thinking of*

Referring to things

■ As the subject of an indirect question, the interrogative pronoun referring to things is **ce qui**, *what*:

je ne sais pas ce qui se passe ici, *I don't know what's happening here*

■ As the object of an indirect question, the interrogative pronoun referring to things is **ce que**, *what*:

explique-moi ce que tu penses, *explain to me what you're thinking*

■ After prepositions, the interrogative pronoun in an indirect question referring to things is **quoi**, *what*:

demande-lui de quoi elle a besoin, *ask her what she needs*

The interrogative pronoun lequel

■ **Lequel** means *which* as an interrogative pronoun. It refers to both people and things and is used in both direct and indirect questions. It agrees with the noun it refers to in gender and number:

	singular	*plural*
masculine	**lequel**	**lesquels**
feminine	**laquelle**	**lesquelles**

Notice that both parts of the word change.

lequel des deux préfères-tu?, *which of the two do you prefer?*

il a répondu à trois questions — lesquelles?, *he's answered three questions—which (ones)?*

je ne sais pas lequel des deux je préfère, *I don't know which of the two I prefer*

■ With the prepositions **à** and **de**, **lequel** forms the following compounds:

	singular	*plural*
masculine	**auquel, duquel**	**auxquels, desquels**
feminine	**à laquelle, de laquelle**	**auxquelles, desquelles**

auquel des trois donnez-vous votre voix?, *which of the three do you give your vote to?*

The interrogative adjective quel

■ The interrogative adjective corresponding to all the above pronouns is **quel**, *which, what*. **Quel** agrees with its noun in gender and number:

	singular	*plural*
masculine	**quel**	**quels**
feminine	**quelle**	**quelles**

avec quelle main l'as-tu fait?, *which hand did you do it with?*

quels gens fréquente-t-il?, *what (kind of) people does he go around with?*

je me demande à quel quai il va arriver, *I wonder which (what) platform it will arrive at*

■ With the verb **être**, **quel** may be divided from its noun by the verb:

quels sont ces gens?, *what (kind of) people are these? (who are these people?)*

► For questions introduced by other question-words see p. 212. For the formation of direct and indirect questions see pp. 211 and 213.

POSSESSIVE PRONOUNS

■ The forms of the possessive pronouns (*mine*, *yours*, etc. in English) are:

masc. sing.	fem. sing.	masc. plural	fem. plural	
le mien	la mienne	les miens	les miennes	*mine*
le tien	la tienne	les tiens	les tiennes	*yours*
le sien	la sienne	les siens	les siennes	*his, hers, its*
le nôtre	la nôtre	les nôtres		*ours*
le vôtre	la vôtre	les vôtres		*yours*
le leur	la leur	les leurs		*theirs*

> **ma mère et la vôtre sont parties ensemble**, *my mother and yours left together*

With **à**, **le/les** becomes **au/aux**; with **de**, **le/les** becomes **du/des**:

> **cet élève est un des miens**, *this pupil is one of mine*

■ The possessive pronouns do not agree with the *owner* of the object, but with the object itself. So **le sien** means either *his* or *hers*, referring to a masculine object, and **la sienne** means either *his* or *hers* referring to a feminine object:

> **mon argent, je l'ai toujours, mais Marie a dépensé tout le sien**, *I've still got my money, but Marie's spent all hers*

■ The possessive pronoun corresponding to **on** and other indefinite pronouns is **le sien**:

> **on s'occupe des siens**, *you look after your own (people)*

■ *It's mine, it's yours*, etc. may also be translated into French by **c'est à moi**, **c'est à toi**, etc. This use of à + disjunctive pronoun is only possible after **être,** where it is extremely common.

There is a slight difference in meaning between **c'est à moi** and **c'est le mien. C'est le mien** distinguishes between objects possessed: 'that one is mine, maybe some other is yours'; **c'est à moi** emphasizes the ownership of the object 'that's mine (so give it me!)'.

DEMONSTRATIVE PRONOUNS

The demonstrative pronouns—English *this (one), that (one), those*—point things out. In French they are **celui,** *this one here; that one there,* specifying, or **ceci/cela,** *this one/that one,* not specifying.

■ The forms of **celui** are:

	masculine	feminine	
singular	**celui**	**celle**	this, that, the one
plural	**ceux**	**celles**	these, those

They agree in gender and number with the noun they refer to.

■ **Celui** does not stand alone. It may be followed by a preposition, by **qui/que** or by **-ci/-là.**

Celui + preposition

The preposition most frequently found after **celui** is **de. Celui de** means *that of* and is the equivalent of the English **'s:**

> **celui de Nicole est cassé,** *Nicole's is broken*
> **la voiture? C'est celle de mon ami,** *the car? It's my friend's*

■ Other prepositions are also found after **celui**:

> **quel tapis? — Celui en laine**, *which carpet?—The woollen one* (*the one in wool*)

Celui à is frequently encountered when shopping:

> **quels abricots? — Ceux à neuf francs**, *which apricots?—The ones at nine francs*

Celui qui, celui que

Celui qui and **celui que** mean *the one who, the one that* or in the plural *those who, those that*. The **qui** and **que** are relative pronouns (see p. 112), so **celui qui** is the subject of its clause and is followed by a verb, **celui que** is the object and is followed by a pronoun or noun subject, and then the verb:

> **celle qui habitait à côté de Jean-Luc a déménagé**, *that woman who lived next to Jean-Luc has moved*
> **lesquels? Ceux que tu trouves difficiles?**, *which? Those you find difficult?*

■ The relatives **à qui** and **dont** are also found after **celui** when the verb that follows takes **à** or **de**:

> **celui à qui je pense**, *the one I'm thinking of* (**penser à**)
> **celle dont tu parles**, *the one you're talking about* (**parler de**)

Celui-ci, celui-là

Celui-ci means *this one*, **celui-là** means *that one* when you are making a specific contrast:

> **celui-ci est bleu, celui-là est plutôt vert**, *this one's blue, that one's more green*

Because **là** is often used to mean *here* as well as *there* in modern French, **celui-là** is losing its ability to point to something at a distance when it is not contrasted, as in the example above, with **celui-ci**. To indicate something at a distance, therefore, **celui là-bas**, *that one over there*, is now often used instead of **celui-là**.

■ **Celui-ci** can also mean *the latter*, **celui-là** *the former*:

> **tu connais Luc et son frère? Alors, celui-ci a demandé de tes nouvelles hier soir**, *you know Luc and his brother? Well, the latter asked (his brother asked) about you last night*

Notice that *the former/the latter* are only used in formal English, whereas **celui-là/celui-ci** can be used with this meaning in French at all levels.

Cela, ça, ceci

Sometimes called neuter demonstratives, **cela** (and its more colloquial form **ça**) means *that* or *this* or *it*, **ceci** means *this*. **Cela/ça** is used much more frequently than **ceci**.

■ **Cela/ça** and **ceci** may refer to ideas, **cela** to one already mentioned, **ceci** to one about to be produced:

> **j'ai entendu tout ce que tu as dit, mais cela est très difficile à comprendre**, *I've heard all you've been saying, but that's (it's) very difficult to understand*
> **ça se comprend!** *that's obvious!*
> **écoutez ceci**, *listen to this*

or they may refer to objects, so far unnamed in the case of **ceci**:

> **je t'ai apporté ceci, c'est un petit cadeau**, *I've brought you this, it's a little present*

already known in the case of **cela / ça**:

> **ça te plaît?**, *do you like it?*

■ Whereas **celui-là** distinguishes between a number of objects, **cela / ça** simply points. Compare:

> **cela m'appartient**, *that's mine* (pointing to a single object)
>
> **celui-là m'appartient**, *that one's mine* (pointing to one among a number of similar objects)

Ce

The pronoun **ce** is a weaker form of **cela / ceci**, used only with **être**, and meaning *it* or *that*:

> **qui est-ce? — C'est moi**, *who's that?—It's me*

Ce becomes **c'** before **e**, **ç** before **a**:

> **ç'a été le plus grand problème**, *that's been the greatest problem*

■ The pronoun **ce** when used as the subject of **être** can also be plural:

> **ce sont des baleines**, *those are whales*

▶ See pp. 224 and 225 for **c'est** versus **il est**.

INDEFINITE PRONOUNS

Indefinite pronouns (*somebody, something, anybody*, etc. in English) all take the third person (**il** form) of the verb in French, as in English. The forms of object pronouns, reflexives, possessives corresponding to indefinite pronouns are also the third person forms (**le, la, lui; se; son, sa, ses; le sien** and their plurals); the corresponding form of the disjunctive is **soi**:

> **chacun doit s'asseoir à sa propre place**,
> *everybody must sit down in his or her own place*

Some indefinites only function as pronouns, some can also be adjectives—see below. See also indefinite adjectives, p. 148.

Used only as pronouns

■ **Chacun** (fem. **chacune**), *each one, everybody*:

> **chacun doit prendre une feuille de papier**,
> *everybody must take a sheet of paper*

■ **Je ne sais quoi**, *something or other*

This phrase is used as if it were a simple pronoun. It may take an adjective, preceded by **de**:

> **elle a dit je ne sais quoi de complètement stupide**,
> *she said something or other completely stupid*

■ **N'importe qui**, *anyone (at all)*:

> **n'importe qui te dira ça**, *anyone (at all) will tell you that*
> **ne le dis pas à n'importe qui**, *don't tell just anyone*

■ **On**, *one, you, we, they, someone, people in general*:

> **on nous regarde**, *somebody's looking at us*
> **qu'est-ce qu'on va faire?**, *what are we going to do?*

▶ See also pp. 103, 109, and (**on** as a substitute for the passive) 34.

■ **Personne**, *nobody, not anybody*:

> **qui est là? — Personne**, *who's there—Nobody*
> **je n'y vois personne**, *I can't see anyone there*

Personne must have a **ne** with an associated verb, as in the second example above. See p. 159.

Any adjective with **personne** follows it, is masculine, and is preceded by **de**:

> **il n'y a personne de compétent**, *there is no one qualified*

■ **Quelque chose**, *something, anything*:

> **tu as vu quelque chose?**, *did you see anything?*
> **oui, il y a quelque chose qui bouge**, *yes, there's something moving*

Any adjective with **quelque chose** follows it, is masculine, and is preceded by **de**:

> **ça doit être quelque chose d'horrible!**, *it must be something horrible!*

The other **chose** compounds behave similarly:

> **autre chose**, *something else*
> **peu de chose**, *little*
> **pas grand-chose**, *not much*

■ **Quelqu'un**, *someone, anybody*:

> **il y a quelqu'un dans la grange**, *there's someone in the barn*
> **est-ce que tu entends quelqu'un?**, *can you hear anybody?*

Quelqu'un has masculine and feminine plural forms (**quelques-uns, quelques-unes**) but no feminine singular form (the masculine must be used even if you are aware that 'someone' is a woman):

> **il vit avec quelqu'un depuis trois ans**, *he's been living with somebody for three years*

The plural form, **quelques-un(e)s**, must have an **en** with its associated verb when it is used as the direct object:

> **ces dames-là? oui, j'en connais quelques-unes**, *those ladies? yes, I know some of them*

Any adjective with **quelqu'un** follows it and is preceded by **de**:

> **je cherche quelqu'un de beau**, *I'm looking for someone handsome*

■ **Quiconque,** *whoever; anybody*:

> **quiconque dit cela, ment!**, *whoever says that is lying!*
> **il joue mieux que quiconque**, *he plays better than anybody*

Qui que ce soit (qui/que) may be used, in rather less formal style, for **quiconque**. See p. 234.

■ **Rien,** *nothing, not anything*:

> **tu entends quelque chose? — Non, rien**, *can you hear anything?—No, nothing*
> **je n'entends absolument rien**, *I can hear absolutely nothing*

Rien must have a **ne** with an associated verb, as in the second example above. See p. 159.

Any adjective with **rien** follows it, is masculine, and is preceded by **de**:

> **ce n'est rien de spécial**, *it's nothing special*

■ **L'un** (fem. **l'une**), *(the) one*:

> **j'ai rencontré l'un d'eux en ville**, *I met one of them in town*
> **l'une chante, l'autre pas**, *one sings, the other doesn't*

As in the second example above, **l'un** is often followed later in the sentence by **l'autre**, *another, the other*. The plural is **les un(e)s … les autres …**

L'un(e) l'autre (plural **les un(e)s les autres**) is used to mean *one another, each other*:

> **ils se détestent l'un l'autre**, *they hate one another*

Used as both pronouns and adjectives

▶ For these indefinites used as adjectives, see p. 148.

■ **Aucun** (fem. **aucune**), *none, not any*:

> **tu as entendu ses disques? — Non, aucun**, *you've heard his records?—No, none of them*
> **il n'en a aucun**, *he hasn't any*

Aucun must have **en** before the verb when it is used as the direct object; it must also have a **ne** with an associated verb, as in the second example above. See p. 159.

Pas un (fem. **pas une**) and **nul** (fem. **nulle**) are found as alternatives to **aucun**, with the same meaning.

■ **Certains** (fem. **certaines**), *some (people)*:

> **certains ont dit qu'il a subtilisé l'argent**, *some people said he pinched the money*
> **certaines d'entre elles ont très bien parlé**, *some of them spoke very well*

Certain(e)s must have **en** before the verb when used as the direct object:

> **j'en connais certains**, *I know some of them*

■ **Plusieurs**, *several (people)*:

> **plusieurs sont venus sans savoir pourquoi**, *several came without knowing why*

Plusieurs must have **en** before the verb when used as the direct object:

> **il en a tué plusieurs**, *he killed several (of them)*

Any adjective with **plusieurs** follows it and is preceded by **de**:

> **il y en a plusieurs de verts**, *there are several green ones*

■ **Tous** (fem. **toutes**), *everybody, all*:

> **je vous connais tous**, *I know you all*
> **elles sont toutes là**, *they are all there*
> **tous sont venus à la réunion**, *all of them came to the meeting*

Tous usually follows the verb, as in the first two examples above, whether it refers to the subject or the object. It stands before the verb when it alone is the subject, as in the third example above.

■ **Tout**, *everything, all*:

> **tout est arrangé**, *all is arranged*
> **j'ai tout fait**, *I've done everything*

Adjectives

In French, adjectives are singular or plural and masculine or feminine according to the noun they refer to. To the basic masculine form **-e** is added to make the adjective feminine, **-s** to make it masculine plural, **-es** to make it feminine plural:

	singular	*plural*
masculine	**un stylo noir**, *a black pen*	**des stylos noirs**
feminine	**une boîte noire**, *a black box*	**des boîtes noires**

An adjective referring to two singular nouns is plural; if they are of different genders the adjective is masculine plural:

> **un complet et une cravate noirs**, *a black suit and tie*

Adjectives usually follow their noun; but see p. 138, position of adjectives.

FEMININE OF ADJECTIVES

Adjectives whose masculine form ends in **-e** remain unchanged in the feminine:

> **un stylo rouge**, *a red pen*
> **une boîte rouge**, *a red box*

otherwise all adjectives add **-e** to form their feminine.

■ Additional changes are made by adjectives with the following endings. Many of these changes are identical to those made by nouns to form their feminines—see p. 93.

masculine adjective	*feminine adjective*
-c	**-que**
public, *public*	**publique**
except:	
blanc, *white*	**blanche**
franc, *frank*	**franche**
grec, *Greek*	**grecque**
sec, *dry*	**sèche**
-er	**-ère**
dernier, *last*	**dernière**
-eur	**-euse**
trompeur, *deceptive*	**trompeuse**
except:	
inférieur, *lower*	**inférieure**
supérieur, *higher*	**supérieure**
intérieur, *inner*	**intérieure**
extérieur, *outer*	**extérieure**
majeur, *major*	**majeure**
mineur, *minor*	**mineure**
meilleur, *better*	**meilleure**
and see **-teur** below	

-f	-ve
informatif, *informative*	**informative**
except:	
bref, *brief*	**brève**
-gu	**-guë** (the tréma, ¨, indicates that the **e** is pronounced separately from the **u**)
aigu, *sharp*	**aiguë**
-teur	**-teuse**: where the adjective is based on the present participle of a verb
menteur, *lying*	**menteuse** (**mentir**, p.p. **mentant**)
	-trice: in all other cases
conservateur, *conservative*	**conservatrice** (**conserver**, p.p. **conservant**).
-x	**-se**
heureux, *happy*	**heureuse**
except:	
doux, *gentle*	**douce**
faux, *false*	**fausse**
roux, *red-haired*	**rousse**
vieux, *old*	**vieille**

■ Adjectives with the following endings double the consonant of their ending before adding **-e**:

masculine	*feminine*
-el	**-elle**
officiel, *official*	**officielle**
-en	**-enne**
ancien, *former*	**ancienne**
-et	**-ette**
net, *clear*	**nette**
except:	
complet, *complete*	**complète**
concret, *concrete*	**concrète**

discret, *discreet*	**discrète**
inquiet, *worried*	**inquiète**
secret, *secret*	**secrète**
-eil	**-eille**
pareil, *similar*	**pareille**
-on	**-onne**
bon, *good*	**bonne**

■ The following adjectives have a special form used before a masculine singular noun beginning with a vowel or 'mute' **h**, and their feminine form is derived from this:

masculine	*masc. before vowel*	*feminine*
beau, *fine*	**bel**	**belle**
fou, *mad*	**fol**	**folle**
mou, *soft*	**mol**	**molle**
nouveau, *new*	**nouvel**	**nouvelle**
vieux, *old*	**vieil**	**vieille**

■ Other adjectives with irregular feminine forms:

masculine	*feminine*
bas, *low*	**basse**
bénin, *benign*	**bénigne**
épais, *thick*	**épaisse**
favori, *favourite*	**favorite**
frais, *fresh*	**fraîche**
gras, *greasy*	**grasse**
gros, *big*	**grosse**
gentil, *nice*	**gentille**
jumeau, *twin*	**jumelle**
las, *tired*	**lasse**
long, *long*	**longue**
malin, *cunning*	**maligne**
nul, *no*	**nulle**
paysan, *peasant*	**paysanne**
sot, *foolish*	**sotte**

■ The following adjectives are usually invariable — they make no agreement at all with either a feminine or a plural noun:

> **châtain**, *chestnut*
> **impromptu**, *impromptu*
> **k(h)aki**, *khaki*
> **marron**, *brown*
> **snob**, *snobbish*

and all compound colour-adjectives:

> **une voiture bleu clair**, *a light blue car*
> **une boîte vert foncé**, *a dark green box*

The following adjectives make plural but no feminine agreements:

> **chic** (m. and f. plural **chics**), *chic*
> **maximum** (m. and f. plural, **maximums**), *maximum*
> **minimum** (m. and f. plural **minimums**), *minimum*

PLURAL OF ADJECTIVES

■ All feminine and most masculine adjectives form their plural by adding **-s** to their singular form. This also applies where the feminine singular is irregular:

	singular	*plural*
masculine	**bon**, *good*	**bons**
feminine	**bonne**	**bonnes**

■ Adjectives ending as follows have irregular masculine plurals. Their feminine plurals are formed regularly by adding **-s** to the feminine singular.

masculine singular	*masculine plural*
-s, -x	no change
gris, *grey*	**gris**
faux, *false*	**faux**

-eau	**-eaux**
beau, *fine*	**beaux**
-al	**-aux**
brutal, *brutal*	**brutaux**
except:	
banal, *trite*	**banals**
fatal, *fatal*	**fatals**
final, *final*	**finals**
naval, *naval*	**navals**

▶ A number of adjectives are invariable, remaining unchanged in both their feminine and their plural forms. See p. 137.

POSITION OF ADJECTIVES

The usual position for an adjective in French is immediately after the noun:

> **une robe verte**, *a green dress*

Two or more adjectives after the noun are joined with **et**:

> **une robe verte et blanche**, *a green and white dress*

Adjectives are also found in front of the noun, however, and some adjectives are almost always found in this position:

> **une jolie robe verte et blanche**, *a pretty green and white dress*

Adjectives that commonly precede are:

> **beau**, *fine*
> **bon**, *good* (and **meilleur**, *better, best*)
> **court**, *short*

gentil, *nice*
grand, *big; tall*
gros, *big*
jeune, *young*
joli, *pretty*
long, *long*
mauvais, *bad* (and **pire**, *worse, worst*)
méchant, *nasty*
nouveau, *new*
petit, *little* (and **moindre**, *less, least*)
vaste, *vast*
vieux, *old*
vilain, *ugly*

If in doubt place these adjectives before the noun, and all others after.

■ Most adjectives can in fact be placed before or after their noun, with a small but distinct difference in meaning. Placing the adjective after the noun indicates an objective distinction, placing it before shows a subjective feeling. So:

> **le long de cette côte s'étire une interminable plage**, *along this coastline stretches an endless beach* (travel agent's language: 'endless' is gushing and imprecise—'that seems as though it might go on for ever'; **une plage interminable**, however, means that the beach is literally or apparently interminable (and therefore boring and tiresome)

This use of adjectives before the noun is very common in modern French writing at all levels to strengthen the emotional content. The effect is often lost in written English: in spoken English we usually get it by stressing the adjective in some way:

> **ces superbes peintures**, *these superb paintings*
> **une fantastique reproduction**, *a fantastic*
> *reproduction*
> **cette magnifique vallée**, *this magnificent valley*
> **d'une rare qualité**, *of a really rare quality*

The adjectives listed on p. 138 above are rarely used as distinguishers: this is why they usually go before the noun. Some adjectives, however, such as colour adjectives, are almost always used to make an objective distinction and so they normally follow the noun.

■ There are some adjectives whose position is completely fixed:

□ Numbers, both cardinal (*one*, *two*, *three*, etc.) and ordinal (*first*, *second*, *third*, etc.), always precede the noun.

> **les trois mousquetaires**, *the three musketeers*
> **le quatrième mousquetaire**, *the fourth musketeer*

But in the following cases where the number follows in English it also follows in French.

> **numéro deux**, *number two*
> **page cinq**, *page five*
> **Henri quatre**, *Henri the Fourth*
> **acte trois**, *act three*

□ Demonstrative, possessive, and interrogative adjectives always precede.

> **cet enfant-là**, *that child*
> **son parapluie**, *his umbrella*
> **quelle difficulté?**, *what difficulty?*

□ Indefinite adjectives like **chaque**, *each*, **tel**, *such*, **autre**, *other*, always precede. See p. 148.

> **une telle personne**, *such a person*
> **chaque enfant**, *each child*

☐ Past participles used as adjectives always follow.

> **un verre cassé**, *a broken glass*

☐ Adjectives of nationality always follow.

> **la révolution française**, *the French revolution*

☐ Scientific and technical adjectives always follow.

> **l'acide chlorhydrique**, *hydrochloric acid*

☐ Adjectives with a qualifying phrase always follow.

> **un bon champignon**, *a good mushroom*
> **un champignon bon à manger**, *an edible mushroom*

■ A small number of adjectives have quite different meanings according to whether they precede or follow the noun. They are:

ancien, *former / ancient*

> **un ancien professeur**, *a former teacher*
> **des meubles anciens**, *very old furniture*

certain, *certain* (= *I'm not sure what*) / *definite, (absolutely) sure*

> **un certain jour de mai**, *a certain day (one day) in May*
> **une date certaine**, *a definite date*

cher, *dear* (= *emotionally important*) / *dear* (= *expensive*)

> **mon cher Charles**, *my dear Charles*
> **une lampe chère**, *an expensive lamp*

dernier, *last (of a sequence) / last* (= *just gone*)

> **le dernier chèque de mon chéquier**, *the last cheque in my chequebook*
> **dimanche dernier**, *last Sunday*

divers, *various/varying*

> **j'ai eu diverses difficultés,** *I've had various difficulties*
> **on m'a donné des réponses diverses,** *I've been given varying replies*

même, *same/very*

> **la même chose,** *the same thing*
> **l'homme même,** *the very man*

Même before the article or before a pronoun means *even*:

> **même cet homme-là,** *even that man*
> **même vous,** *even you*

pauvre, *poor (= to be pitied)/poor (= not rich)*

> **ce pauvre enfant!,** *that poor child!*
> **une famille pauvre,** *a poor family*

propre, *own/clean*

> **mes propres mains,** *my own hands*
> **les mains propres,** *clean hands*

seul, *only/alone*

> **la seule solution,** *the only solution*
> **le roi seul a le droit de décider,** *the king alone has the right to decide* (this use is the equivalent of 'only the king', and **seul le roi** is equally possible)

vrai, *real (= genuine)/true (= not fictitious)*

> **un vrai mystère,** *a real mystery*
> **une histoire vraie,** *a true story*

COMPARATIVE AND SUPERLATIVE OF ADJECTIVES

■ English has two ways to form the comparative and superlative of adjectives:

> *fine*: *finer* (comparative), *finest* (superlative)
> *difficult*: *more difficult* (comparative), *most difficult* (superlative)

French forms the comparative and superlative in one way only, with **plus** (comparative) and **le/la/les plus** (superlative):

> **beau, plus beau, le plus beau**, *fine, finer, finest*

> **la voile est un plus beau sport que le tennis**, *sailing is a finer sport than tennis*
> **c'est le plus beau sport du monde**, *it's the finest sport in the world*

> **difficile, plus difficile, le plus difficule**, *difficult, more difficult, most difficult*

> **c'est une activité encore plus difficile**, *it's an even more difficult activity*
> **c'est l'activité la plus difficile**, *it's the most difficult activity*

■ The comparative or superlative comes in the same position, before or after the noun, that the adjective itself would take, and agrees in the same way as an ordinary adjective does. Notice that where it comes after the noun, the superlative adjective has its own definite article, independently of any article that already stands with the noun:

> **cette activité la plus difficile de toutes**, *this most difficult of all activities*

A superlative adjective immediately after a possessive (**mon, ma, mes; ton, ta, tes,** etc.) drops its definite article:

> **sa plus jolie jupe**, *her prettiest skirt*

■ The following comparative and superlative adjectives are exceptional:

> **bon, meilleur, le meilleur**, *good, better, best*
>
> **mauvais, plus mauvais, le plus mauvais,** or **mauvais, pire, le pire** (**pire, le pire** are less common. They are mainly used in some set phrases: **le remède est pire que le mal**, *the cure is worse than the disease*)
>
> **petit, plus petit, le plus petit**, *small, (physically) smaller, smallest,* or **petit, moindre, le moindre**, *little, less* (= *of less importance*), *least*

■ Comparisons, as well as being expressed by **plus ... que,** *more ... than*, can also be expressed by:

> **moins ... que**, *less ... than*
>
> **ton journal est moins intéressant que le mien**, *your paper's less interesting than mine*
>
> **aussi ... que**, *as ... as*
>
> **elle est aussi riche que son père**, *she's as rich as her father*
>
> **pas aussi** (or **pas si**) **... que**, *not as ... as*
>
> **elle n'est pas (aus)si riche que son grand-père**, *she's not as rich as her grandfather*

■ *Than* after a comparative is **que**:

> **vous êtes plus jeune qui moi**, *you're younger than me*

As after a comparative is also **que**:

> **elle n'est pas si vieille que lui**, *she's not as old as him*

In after a superlative is **de**:

> **le plus grand bâtiment du monde**, *the biggest building in the world*

By with either a comparative or a superlative is **de**:

> **il est de beaucoup le plus beau**, *he's by far the most handsome*

■ **Le/la/les moins** can also be used, like **le/la/les plus**, as a superlative:

> **l'enfant le moins gâté**, *the least spoiled child*

■ Where **plus** and **moins** are used to compare nouns rather than adjectives they are followed by **de**:

> **tu as plus de force que moi**, *you have more strength than I*
> **la ville a moins d'habitants qu'auparavant**, *the town has fewer inhabitants than formerly*

To express equal quantity **autant de**, *as much as*, is used:

> **elle a autant d'argent que son petit ami**, *she has as much money as her boyfriend*

More than, *less than* plus a quantity is also **plus de**, **moins de**:

> **il a plus de soixante ans**, *he's more than sixty*

■ *More and more* is **de plus en plus**, *less and less* **de moins en moins**:

> **le temps devient de plus en plus orageux**, *the weather's getting more and more stormy*
> **j'ai de moins en moins d'argent**, *I've less and less money*

▶ For the use of the subjunctive in a clause following a superlative, see p. 47.

DEMONSTRATIVE, POSSESSIVE, AND INTERROGATIVE ADJECTIVES

Demonstrative adjectives (*this*, *that* in English) and possessive adjectives (*my*, *your*, *his*, *her*, etc. in English) stand in exactly the same relationship to nouns as do definite and indefinite articles. They are in fact sometimes known as demonstrative and possessive articles.

■ The demonstrative adjective in French is **ce** (masculine singular), **cet** (masculine singular before a vowel or 'mute' **h**), **cette** (feminine singular), **ces** (plural):

> **ce jeune homme**, *this young man*
> **cet homme**, *this man*
> **cette fille**, *this girl*
> **ces gens**, *these people*

Where it is necessary to differentiate between *this* and *that*, **-ci** and **-là** are added to the following noun:

> **ce jeune homme-ci**, *this young man*
> **ces gens-là**, *those people*

However, just as French tends to use **là**, *there*, much more than **ici**, *here*, so **ce ... -là** is used in modern French in many cases where English would use *this*, with **ce ... là-bas** used for the more distant object:

> **tu sais quel train tu prends? Celui-là? — Non, ce train là-bas**, *do you know which train you're getting? This one?—No, that train (there)*

■ The possessive adjectives are:

with masc. sing. noun	with fem. sing. noun	with plur. noun	
mon	**ma**	**mes**	*my*
ton	**ta**	**tes**	*your*
son	**sa**	**ses**	*his, her, its*
	notre	**nos**	*our*
	votre	**vos**	*your*
	leur	**leurs**	*their*

Mon, ton, and **son** are also used before a feminine singular noun beginning with a vowel or 'mute' **h**.

> **c'est ma cassette**, *it's my cassette*
> **c'est ton orange**, *it's your orange* (**orange** is feminine)
> **c'est son pullover**, *it's his/her pullover*

Notice that **son, sa, ses**, like the rest of the possessives, have the gender of the object possessed, not of the person owning it. So **son pullover** is *his* or *her pullover*, **sa cassette** *his* or *her cassette*. Where it is necessary to differentiate, **à lui/à elle** are added:

> **c'est sa cassette à lui**, *it's <u>his</u> cassette*

■ The interrogative adjective in French is **quel?**, *which, what?* It agrees in gender and number with the noun that follows:

	singular	plural
masculine	**quel**	**quels**
feminine	**quelle**	**quelles**

> **quelle robe vas-tu porter?**, *which dress are you going to wear?*

Quel can be used to introduce an indirect question:

> **je ne sais pas quelle robe porter**, *I don't know what dress to wear*
>
> **je me demande quelle robe Sophie va porter**, *I wonder what dress Sophie will wear*

■ **Quel …!** may also be an exclamation, meaning in the singular *what a …!*, *what …!*, in the plural *what …!*

> **quel bel enfant!**, *what a lovely child!*
> **quelle chance!**, *what luck!*
> **quelles vacances formidables!**, *what terrific holidays!*

INDEFINITE ADJECTIVES

Indefinite adjectives, as a group, include in English such words as *several, certain, such*. The indefinite adjectives in French are:

> **aucun, nul**, *no, not any*
> **autre**, *other*
> **certain**, *certain*
> **chaque**, *each*
> **même**, *same*
> **plusieurs**, *several*
> **quelque**, *some, any*
> **tel**, *such*
> **tout** (singular) *all, the whole of*; (plural) *all*; *every*

Chaque has no plural form, **plusieurs** no singular form. **Plusieurs** is unchanged in both masculine and feminine; **tel** and **tout** decline as follows:

	singular	*plural*
masculine	**tel; tout**	**tels; tous**
feminine	**telle; toute**	**telles; toutes**

Aucun and **nul** take **ne** with their verb, like negative adverbs: see p. 159.

■ **Chaque, plusieurs, quelque, aucun, nul,** and **certains** (plural) are used without preceding article:

> **chaque employé recevra la même somme,** *each worker will be paid the same amount*
> **plusieurs d'entre eux sont là,** *several of them are there*
> **j'y vois quelques problèmes,** *I can see some problems there*
> **c'est à cause de certaines difficultés,** *it's because of certain difficulties*

■ **Tout** has the article following, as with *all* in English (but unlike the English usage with *every*):

> **tout le temps,** *all the time*
> **tous les soirs,** *every evening*

In the singular **tout** may be used without article to mean *all, any*:

> **cela exclut tout progrès dans cette affaire,** *that excludes any progress in this matter*

■ **Autre** and **tel** stand after the article like other adjectives. Notice that this is not the case with *such* in English:

> **les autres hommes,** *the other men*
> **un autre homme,** *another man*
> **un tel homme,** *such a man*

Such may also be used in English adverbially to qualify another adjective: *she has such big eyes.* In French this must be the adverb form **tellement,** or **si,** both of which mean *such* or *so*:

> **ses yeux sont tellement grands,** *her eyes are so big*
> **elle a de si grands yeux,** *she has such big eyes*

■ **Même** has four meanings according to position:

☐ Before the article, *even*

>**même son secrétaire le dit**, *even his secretary says so*

☐ Before the noun, or after the verb, *same*

>**c'est exactement la même chose**, *it's exactly the same thing*
>**ces deux filles sont toujours les mêmes**, *those two girls are always the same*

☐ After the noun, *very*

>**ce sont les paroles mêmes du président**, *they are the president's very words*

☐ Attached to a pronoun with a hyphen, *self*

>**il l'a fait lui-même**, *he did it himself*

NOUNS USED ADJECTIVALLY (ATTRIBUTIVE NOUNS)

English frequently uses nouns as adjectives: *a coffee pot, a steel saucepan, a box girder, a cat flap*. These imply something like 'used for', 'made from', 'in the form of', 'used by'. In French the adjectival (or attributive) noun is placed after the main noun, and joined to it with a preposition which makes clear this relationship. The prepositions used are **de**, **à**, and **en**:

de

☐ *of, appropriate for, belonging to*

>**un match de tennis**, *a tennis match* (= *a match of tennis*)

la route de Manieu, *the Manieu road* (= *the road appropriate for Manieu*)

les feuilles d'automne, *autumn leaves* (= *the leaves of autumn*)

des poulets de batterie, *battery hens* (= *belonging to a battery*)

☐ *for the purpose of*

une salle d'attente, *a waiting room* (= *a room for the purpose of waiting*)

un effet de choc, *a shock effect* (= *an effect for the purpose of shocking*)

à

☐ *to contain, intended for*

ᵗ **un pot à café**, *a coffee pot* (= *a pot to contain coffee*. Compare **un pot de café**, *a pot of coffee*)

une boîte aux lettres, *a letter box* (= *a box intended for letters*)

Verbal nouns (the *-ing* form in English, the infinitive in French) use **à** with this meaning to transform themselves into adjectives:

une salle à manger, *a dining room* (= *a room intended for eating*)

une machine à laver, *a washing machine* (= *a machine intended for washing*)

☐ *using, employing*

une poutre à caisson, *a box girder* (= *a girder using a box shape*)

un moulin à vent, *a windmill* (= *a mill that uses wind*)

☐ *with, possessing*

un chien à pedigree, *a pedigree dog* (= *a dog possessing pedigree*)

en

☐ *made from*

> **une casserole en acier**, *a steel saucepan* (= a
> saucepan made from steel)
> **un bracelet en or**, *a gold bracelet* (= a bracelet
> made from gold)

De is sometimes used in this way, too:

> **une barre de fer**, *an iron bar*

☐ *in the form of*

> **un escalier en spirale**, *a spiral staircase* (= a
> staircase in the form of a spiral)

■ Sometimes, especially with modern words, the
adjectival noun simply follows the main one, without any
preposition, though often with a hyphen:

> **une cocotte-minute**, *a pressure cooker* ('minute
> casserole')
> **une bande-annonce**, *a film trailer* ('advertisement
> reel')

Adverbs

FORMATION OF ADVERBS

Adverbs formed from adjectives

■ Most French adverbs are formed by adding **-ment** to the feminine form of the adjective:

> **égal**, *equal* → feminine: **égale**
> → adverb: **également**, *equally*

■ If the masculine form of the adjective ends in a vowel, **-ment** is added to this masculine form:

> **vrai**, *real* → **vraiment**, *really*
> **forcé**, *forced* → **forcément**, *'forcedly'*, *necessarily*

Nouveau, mou, and **fou,** however, base their adverbs on their differing feminine forms **nouvelle, molle,** and **folle:**

> **nouveau** → **nouvellement**, *newly*
> **mou** → **mollement**, *softly*
> **fou** → **follement**, *madly*

■ Adjectives ending **-ent** and **-ant** form adverbs ending **-emment** and **-amment** (both pronounced as if they were spelled **-amment**):

> récent → récemment, *recently*
> constant → constamment, *constantly*

Exceptions: **lent → lentement**, *slowly*; **présent → présentement**, *presently*

■ A number of adjectives that do not end in **é** follow the pattern of **forcément**:

> aveugle → aveuglément, *blindly*
> commun → communément, *communally*
> confus → confusément, *confusedly*
> énorme → énormément, *enormously*
> exprès → expressément, *explicitly*
> impuni, *unpunished* →impunément, *with impunity, scot-free*
> intense, *intense* →intensément, *intensively*
> précis → précisément, *precisely*
> profond → profondément, *deeply*

■ The following adverbs are completely irregular in the way they are formed from their adjectives:

> bon → bien, *well*
> bref → brièvement, *briefly*
> continu → continûment, *continuously*
> gai → gaiement, *gaily*
> gentil → gentiment, *kindly*
> mauvais → mal, *badly*
> meilleur → mieux, *better*
> moindre → moins, *less*
> petit → peu, *little*
> traître → traîtreusement, *treacherously*

Adverbs not formed from adjectives

There are also many adverbs in French which are not formed from adjectives, mostly short words like **ainsi, donc, dedans**:

> **ainsi c'est entendu?**, *so it's agreed?*

Some of these relate to conjunctions:

> **ainsi**, *thus*, conjunction → **ainsi**, *so*, adverb

some to prepositions:

> **dans**, *in*, preposition → **dedans**, *inside*, adverb

some are independent:

> **donc**, *then*, adverb

Adverb alternatives

■ Adjectives are used as adverbs in a number of fixed expressions:

bas, haut	**parler bas, parler haut**, *speak softly/loudly*
bon, mauvais	**sentir bon, sentir mauvais**, *smell good/bad*
cher	**coûter cher, payer cher**, *cost/pay a lot*
court	**s'arrêter court, couper court**, *stop/cut short*
dur	**travailler dur**, *work hard*
juste / faux	**chanter juste, chanter faux**, *sing in/out of tune*
net	**refuser net**, *refuse point blank*

■ Adverb phrases commonly substitute for the longer and more cumbersome adverbs, and must be used where the adjective has no corresponding adverb, such as **content**, *happy*, *content*:

> **il me regarda d'un air content**, *he looked at me contentedly*
>
> **— Ah non, dit-il d'une voix triste**, *'Oh no,' he said sadly*
>
> **elle répondit à voix basse**, *she answered softly*
>
> **je l'ai fait avec soin**, *I did it carefully*
>
> **le régiment s'est battu avec beaucoup de courage**, *the regiment fought very courageously*
>
> **elle l'a fait sans hésitation**, *she did it unhesitatingly*

POSITION OF ADVERBS

Adverbs describe or modify a verb:

> **elle joue bien**, *she plays well* (adverb: **bien**)

or an adjective:

> **cela est complètement différent**, *that's completely different* (adverb: **complètement**)

or another adverb:

> **oui, très probablement**, *yes, very probably* (modifying adverb: **très**)

■ With adjectives and adverbs the modifying adverb stands immediately in front of the word it modifies, as in English. See the last two examples above.

■ With verbs:

□ In simple tenses adverbs usually stand immediately after the verb.

> **je connais intimement toute cette famille**, *I know all that family intimately*

□ In compound tenses adverbs follow the past participle if they take the stress.

> **je l'ai vu finalement**, *I saw him, in the end*
> **je lui ai finalement parlé**, *I finally spoke to him*

In practice this means that adverbs of place and precise adverbs of time (**aujourd'hui, demain, hier**, etc.) almost always stand after the past participle:

> **elle l'a mis là, sur le plancher**, *she's put it there, on the floor*
> **on l'a fait hier**, *we did it yesterday*

and short adverbs of degree (**bien, beaucoup, trop**, etc.) or imprecise adverbs of time (**déjà, souvent, bientôt**, etc.) stand before the past participle:

> **tu l'as très bien expliqué**, *you explained it very well*
> **il est déjà arrivé**, *he's already arrived*

☐ With a dependent infinitive the above points about adverbs with the past participle also apply.

> **je vais le faire finalement**, *I'm finally going to do it*
> **je vais finalement lui parler**, *I'm finally going to speak to him*

■ Adverbs, especially those of time and place, may be placed at the head of their clause for emphasis, as they sometimes are in English:

> **partout on voyait des coquelicots**, *everywhere poppies could be seen*
> **jamais je n'aurais fait cela**, *I'd never have done that*

■ Interrogative adverbs stand at the head of their clause, of course:

> **quand reviendra-t-elle?**, *when will she come back?*

▶ For the word order after interrogative adverbs, see p. 212.

COMPARATIVE AND SUPERLATIVE OF ADVERBS

In English the comparative and superlative are:

> *easily*→comparative: *more easily*
> superlative: *most easily*

In French the comparative and superlative of adverbs are formed in a similar way to those of adjectives (for which see p. 143):

> **facilement**, *easily*
> *comparative* **plus facilement**, *more easily*
> *superlative* **le plus facilement**, *most easily*

> **c'est comme ça que tu le feras le plus facilement**,
> *that's the way you'll do it most easily*

■ The superlative adverb always starts **le** (never **la** or **les**):

> **c'est elle qui le fera le plus facilement**, *she's the one who will do it most easily*

■ As with adjectives

> **moins ... que**, *less ... than*
> **aussi ... que**, *as ... as*
> **si ... que**, *as* (after a negative)

can be used to form comparatives in the same way as **plus ... que**:

> **elle part en vacances moins souvent que toi**, *she goes on holiday less often than you*
> **il ne conduit pas si vite que toi**, *he doesn't drive as fast as you*

Le moins ..., *the least ...*, can also be used in a similar way to **le plus ...**, *the most ...*, to form a superlative:

> **celui qui le fait le moins bien**, *the one who does it least well*

■ The following adverbs have irregular comparatives and superlatives:

> **beaucoup**, *much*   **plus, le plus**, *more, the most*
> **bien**, *well*   **mieux, le mieux**, *better, the best*
> **peu**, *little*   **moins, le moins**, *less, the least*

The comparative adverb **pis**, *worse*, corresponding to the comparative adjective **pire,** is now only used in a few set expressions:

> **tant pis pour lui!,** *so much the worse for him!*

NEGATIVE ADVERBS

The negative adverbs in French are

> **aucun,** *no, none*
> **guère,** *hardly*
> **jamais,** *never*
> **ni,** *neither; nor*
> **nul,** *no*
> **nulle part,** *nowhere*
> **nullement,** *in no way*
> **pas,** *not*
> **personne,** *nobody*
> **plus,** *no longer*
> **que,** *only*
> **rien,** *nothing*

Negating a verb

The normal position for all the negative adverbs is after the verb in simple tenses, and before the past participle in compound tenses. In addition, they all have **ne** before the verb and any accompanying object pronouns. **Ne** becomes **n'** before a vowel or 'mute' **h:**

> **je ne le lui donne jamais,** *I never give it to him*
> **je n'ai rien dit,** *I haven't said anything*

■ **Nulle part** and **personne** normally come after the past participle in compound tenses:

> **ils n'ont vu personne,** *they haven't seen anyone*
> **on ne le trouve nulle part,** *it is not found anywhere*

■ Ni

□ With two objects: the **ni** is repeated in front of each object. Any pronoun object must be a disjunctive (see p. 111)

> **je n'ai rencontré ni lui ni sa femme**, *I met neither him nor his wife*

□ With two subjects: the **ni** is repeated in front of each subject. Any pronoun subject must be a disjunctive (see p. 111). The verb is usually plural

> **ni lui ni sa femme n'étaient là**, *neither he nor his wife was (were) there*

□ With two verbs: the **ne** is repeated

> **il ne fume ni ne boit**, *he neither smokes nor drinks*

Neither without *nor* is **non plus**:

> **moi non plus**, *me neither!*
> **je ne l'ai pas vu non plus**, *I haven't seen him either*

■ Que, *only*, qualifying an object stands in front of the object. A pronoun object must be a disjunctive (see p. 111):

> **je n'aime que lui**, *I love only him*
> **je n'ai vraiment regardé que l'acteur principal**, *I only really looked at the main actor*

Que can also be made to qualify a verb by using the verb as an infinitive in the construction **ne faire que**:

> **cet enfant ne fait que crier**, *that child only cries (does nothing but cry)*

Que can itself be negated with **pas**:

> **il n'y a pas que Pierre qui soit invité**, *it's not only Pierre who's been invited*

■ **Aucun** and **nul** are actually adjectives, agreeing with the noun they stand in front of. They are used only in the singular; **nul** has the feminine form **nulle**.

In all other respects **aucun** and **nul** are like the other negative adverbs.

■ **Personne, rien, ni … ni…, aucun …** and **nul …** can stand as the subject of the sentence. The **ne** still appears before the verb (but beware—there is no **pas!**):

> **personne ne l'a entendu,** *nobody's heard him*

See indefinite pronouns, pp. 127 ff.

Negating an infinitive

■ With an infinitive both the **ne** and the negative adverb stand in front of the infinitive and its pronoun objects:

> **je peux ne pas venir,** *I may possibly not come* (as opposed to **je ne peux pas venir,** *I can't come*)

except in the case of those negative adverbs which follow the past participle (**personne, nulle part, ni, que, aucun, nul**), which also follow the infinitive:

> **je suis désolé de ne voir personne,** *I'm very sorry not to see anyone*
> **j'espère ne trouver ni difficultés ni problèmes,** *I hope to find neither difficulties nor problems*

■ **Sans** + infinitive can stand with all the negative adverbs, without a **ne**:

> **sans rien voir,** *without seeing anything*

Double negative adverbs

Plus and **jamais** can qualify another negative adverb. They stand in front of it:

> **je ne vois plus personne**, *I don't see anybody any more*
> **je n'achète jamais rien**, *I never buy anything*

Negatives with other parts of the sentence

■ *Not* with parts of the sentence other than the verb is either **pas** or **non**, or the stronger **non pas**. **Ne** does not appear in this case:

> **je veux des pommes, et non pas des pommes de terre!**, *I want apples, not potatoes!*

■ Most of the negative adverbs can be used without **ne** where no verb is expressed:

> **qui a téléphoné? — Personne**, *who phoned?—Nobody*
> **qu'est-ce que tu entends? — Plus rien**, *what can you hear?—Nothing any more*

Omission of ne and pas

■ **Ne** is omitted extremely frequently in spoken French:

> **Jean-Luc? Connais pas!**, *Jean-Luc? Don't know him!*
> **elle vient ce soir? — Oh, je sais pas**, *is she coming tonight?—Oh, I don't know*

■ **Pas** is omitted in literary French with the verbs **pouvoir, savoir, oser** + infinitive

> **je ne savais comment répondre**, *I did not know how to reply*

Non-negative ne

A non-negative **ne** is used in careful speech in clauses dependent on a number of expressions, mostly involving the subjunctive. The commonest are:

- Verbs of fearing: **avoir peur que, craindre que**

> **j'ai peur qu'elle ne soit déjà là**, *I'm afraid she may be there already*

- Conjunctions: **avant que, à moins que, de peur que, de crainte que**

> **je l'ai fait de peur qu'elle ne le fasse elle-même**, *I did it for fear she (in case she) might do it herself*

- Comparisons: **plus ... que, moins ... que**

> **il est moins habile que vous ne pensez**, *he is less clever than you think*

This **ne** has no negative meaning and is not used in everyday spoken French.

▶ See uses of the subjunctive, pp. 41 ff.

Prepositions

Prepositions—words like *in*, *on*, *over*—stand in front of a noun or pronoun to relate it to the rest of the sentence:

> **il chante toujours dans la salle de bain**, *he always sings in the bathroom* (preposition: **dans**, *in*)

■ Prepositions can also stand in front of a verb—*without looking*, *by singing*. In English this part of a verb is the *-ing* form. In French it is the infinitive:

> **sans regarder**, *without looking*

except with the preposition **en**, which is followed by a present participle:

> **en chantant**, *whilst singing*

■ The prepositions **à** and **de** combine with the definite article to form **au**, **aux** and **du**, **des**. See p. 77.

■ The prepositions **à**, **de**, and **en** are usually repeated if they refer to more than one noun or pronoun. This is often not the case in English:

> **j'ai parlé à lui et à ses voisins**, *I spoke to him and his neighbours*

ALPHABETICAL LIST OF FRENCH PREPOSITIONS AND THEIR USE

The use of prepositions differs considerably from language to language. Below we give an alphabetical list of those French prepositions that may give difficulty, with their main and subsidiary meanings and examples of their use. The principal meaning (or meanings) is given first, with other meanings following in alphabetical order.

In addition, on p. 185 there is an alphabetical list of English prepositions with their various French equivalents, for cross-reference to the French list.

à, *at*

at (place)

> **on se retrouve à la gare routiere**, *we'll meet at the bus station*
> **à la maison**, *at home*
> **à l'école**, *at school*
> **au travail**, *at work*

at (time)

> **à midi et à une heure**, *at noon and at one o'clock*
> **au crépuscule**, *at twilight*
> **à l'aube**, *at dawn*
> **à Noël**, *at Christmas*

at (numbers)

> **à cent kilomètres à l'heure**, (*at*) *100 km. an hour*
> **à très peu de distance**, *at a very little distance*
> **ceux à vingt francs**, *those at 20 francs*

belonging to (English uses the possessive pronoun):

> **c'est à lui** (= it belongs to him), *it's his*

▶ See p. 123.

by

> **tu le reconnaîtras à sa moustache**, *you'll recognize him by his moustache*
> **des dentelles faites à la main** (= by hand), *hand-made lace*
> **cela se vend au kilo**, *we sell that by the kilo*

for (English uses an attributive noun)

> **un réservoir à essence** (= a tank for petrol), *a petrol tank*
>
> **un verre à vin** (= a glass for wine), *a wineglass* (compare **un verre de vin**, *a glass of wine*)

from

> **il l'a pris à ton frère**, *he took it from your brother* (and similarly **arracher à**, *snatch from*, **acheter à**, *buy from*, **boire à**, *drink from*, **cacher à**, *hide from*, **emprunter à**, *borrow from*, **voler à**, *steal from*)

in (place)

> **à la campagne**, *in the country* (but **en ville**, *in town*)
>
> **à la main**, *in my* (*her, your, etc.*) *hand*
>
> **au lit**, *in bed*
>
> **au ciel**, *in the sky*
>
> **au soleil**, *in the sun*
>
> **à Marseille**, *in Marseilles*
>
> **aux États-Unis**, *in the United States*
>
> **au Mexique**, *in Mexico* (but **en** with feminine singular countries: **en France**)

in (time)

> **au petit matin**, *in the early morning* (but without an adjective '*in*' with parts of the day is just **le**: **le matin**, *in the morning*; **l'après-midi**, *in the afternoon*; **le soir**, *in the evening*)
>
> **au XXᵉ siècle**, *in the twentieth century*
>
> **au mois de mai**, *in* (*the month of*) *May* (but **en mai**, *in May*)
>
> **au printemps**, *in spring* (but **en** with the other seasons: **en été**, *in summer*)
>
> **à son tour**, *in* (*his*) *turn*

in (manner)

> **à voix basse**, *in a soft voice*
> **des champignons à la grecque**, *mushrooms cooked the Greek way*
> **des tripes à la mode de Caen**, *Caen-style tripe*

on

> **au menu**, *on the menu*
> **ces peintures au mur**, *those paintings on the wall*
> **marqué au front**, *marked on the forehead*
> **à bicyclette, à pied, à cheval**, *on a bicycle (by bicycle), on foot, on horseback*
> **à droite/gauche**, *on the right/left*
> **à la page dix-huit**, *on page 18*

to

> **je vais à la boulangerie**, *I'm going to the baker's*
> **elle va à Paris, aux États-Unis, au Portugal**, *she's going to Paris, the USA, Portugal* (but **en** with feminine singular countries: **elle va en Italie**, *she's going to Italy*)
> **j'ai parlé à ton professeur**, *I've spoken to your teacher*
> **du matin au soir**, *from morning to (till) night*

using (English usually has an attributive noun)

> **un moteur à essence** (= using petrol), *a petrol engine*
> **un moulin à vent** (= using wind), *a windmill*
> **une locomotive à vapeur** (= using steam), *a steam locomotive*

with (= *containing, having*—English may use an attributive noun)

> **une pâté aux truffes** (= a pâté with truffles), *truffle pâté*
> **un chien à pedigree** (= a dog with a pedigree), *a pedigree dog*

l'homme au parapluie, *the man with the umbrella*
la femme aux yeux verts, *the woman with green eyes*

▶ For uses of **à** with verbs see p. 56.

▶ For **à** used after adjectives, nouns, and adverbs see p. 51.

à part, *except*

▶ See **au dehors de**, below.

à travers, *through*

▶ See **par**, p. 180.

après, *after*

after (time)

> **après trois heures**, *after three o'clock*
> **après la guerre**, *after the war*

after (place)

> **la troisième maison après la mairie**, *the third house after the town hall*
> **elle court après lui**, *she's running after him*

according to (notice the **d'**)

> **d'après Le Figaro**, *according to Le Figaro*

▶ For **après** + perfect infinitive (*after …ing*), see p. 53.

au-dehors de, *outside*

outside

> **ce chien reste au-dehors de la maison**, *that dog stays outside the house*

The shorter form **hors de** locates less precisely:

> **ceux qui habitent hors de la ville**, *those who live (somewhere) outside the town*

Hors de also means *out of*:

> **elle était hors d'haleine**, *she was out of breath*

and, in literary usage, **hors** means *except*:

> **nous y sommes tous allés hors lui**, *we all went except him*

Except is, however, now more usually **à part**:

> **personne à part sa mère**, *no one except her mother*

au-dessous de, *under(neath), below*

▶ See **sous**, p. 183.

au-dessus de, *over*

over, above (physically)

> **le ciel au-dessus de la montagne**, *the sky over (above) the mountains*

Over, above with motion is **par-dessus**:

> **sauter par-dessus un obstacle**, *to leap over an obstacle*

Where *over* implies *touching* it is **sur**:

> **une serviette sur le bras**, *with a towel over his arm*

above, over (= *more than*)

> **ne paie pas au-dessus de cent francs**, *don't pay above (more than) 100 francs*

auprès de, *beside*

beside (nearness)

> **elle se tenait auprès du lit,** *she was standing beside the bed*

beside (= *compared to*)

> **son frère jumeau n'est rien auprès de lui,** *his twin brother is nothing beside (compared to) him*

avant, *before*

before (time)

> **avant le commencement du jeu,** *before the beginning of the match*
> **avant de sortir,** *before going out* (note the **de** before an infinitive)

before (place in a sequence of places)

> **vous descendez avant Genève?,** *are you getting out before Geneva?*

The older, formal use of *before* to mean *in front of* is **devant**:

> **il s'agenouilla devant l'autel,** *he knelt before the altar*

avec, *with*

with (= *together with*)

> **tu viens avec nous?,** *are you coming with us?*

with (= *by means of*)

> **tu n'y arriveras pas avec un tire-bouchon,** *you won't manage it with a corkscrew*

chez, *at X's*

at (or to) the house or shop of (English usually uses a
possessive)

> **on va chez l'épicier**, *we're going to the grocer's*
> **on se voit chez Chantal**, *see you at Chantal's*
> **faites comme chez vous**, *make yourself at home*

with (= *as far as X is concerned*)

> **c'est une habitude chez elle**, *with her it's a
> habit*

among

> **chez les Esquimaux on ne joue pas beaucoup au
> tennis**, *not much tennis is played among the
> Eskimos*

in (*the works of*)

> **on ne trouve pas ce mot chez Racine**, *that word
> isn't found in Racine*

contre, *against*

against (in both concrete and abstract senses)

> **l'échelle est contre le garage**, *the ladder is
> against the garage*
> **nous sommes tous contre la guerre**, *we are all
> against war*

for

> **tu veux échanger ça contre mon tourne-disques?**,
> *do you want to exchange that for my record
> player?*

dans, *in*

in, into (place)

> **on va dans le jardin**, *we're going into the garden*
> **il y a deux hommes dans sa vie**, *there are two men in her life*

in (time, = *at the end of*)

> **je serai de retour dans dix minutes**, *I'll be back in ten minutes* (= *ten minutes from now*)

> *In* = *within the space of* is **en**:

> **je le ferai en dix minutes**, *I'll do it in* (*within the space of*) *ten minutes*

from

> **je l'ai pris dans le tiroir**, *I took it from the drawer*

▶ See also **à**, *from*, p. 166. The French have in mind the original position of the object, from which it is then taken, snatched, etc.

de, *of*

of (possession or relation—English often uses a possessive or an attributive noun)

> **la voiture de Pierre**, *Pierre's car* (*the car of Pierre*)
> **la première femme de mon oncle**, *my uncle's first wife* (*the first wife of my uncle*)
> **la porte du jardin**, *the garden gate* (*the gate of the garden*)
> **la route de Versailles**, *the Versailles road* (*the road of Versailles*)
> **une partie de plaisir**, *a pleasure party* (*a party of pleasure*)

les vacances de Noël, the Christmas holidays (the holidays of Christmas)

of (= *containing*)

un verre de vin, a glass of wine

of (appositional, = *that is*)

au mois de septembre, in the month of September (the month that is September)

la ville de Paris, the city of Paris

about (= *concerning*)

elle est folle de ses animaux, she's mad about her animals

by

elle est Française de naissance, she's French by birth

il arriva accompagné de sa femme, he arrived accompanied by his wife

il a été blessé d'une balle, he has been hit by a bullet (See p. 33 for the use of **de** with the passive)

from

d'où vient-il?, where has he come from?

il revient de Paris, he's just come back from Paris

de temps en temps, from time to time

elle est différente de sa sœur, she's different from her sister

in (manner)

d'une voix tremblante, in a trembling voice (but à voix basse/haute, in a low/loud voice)

d'une manière impolie, in a rude manner

d'une façon stupide, in a stupid way

Similarly,

d'un air fâché, with an angry look

in (after a superlative or superlative-type word—see p. 145)

> **le meilleur du monde**, *the best in the world*
> **le premier de sa classe**, *the first in its class*

made of (English usually uses an attributive noun)

> **un coussin de soie**, *a silk cushion* (*a cushion made of silk*)
> **un chapeau de paille**, *a straw hat* (*a hat made of straw*)

than (with a quantity following a comparison)

> **plus de cinq fois**, *more than five times*
> **les enfants de moins de treize ans**, *children below (of less than) thirteen years*

to

> **tu es libre de supposer n'importe quoi**, *you are free to assume anything at all*

with

> **il est couvert de boue**, *he's covered with mud*
> **elle pleure de joie**, *she is weeping with joy*
> **il nous questionna d'un air soupçonneux**, *he questioned us with a suspicious look*

De is also used, with no equivalent word in English, in the following cases.

■ After expressions of quantity (this includes **un million**, *million*, and **un milliard**, *billion*, but not other numbers):

> **beaucoup de monde**, *a lot of people*
> **trop de questions**, *too many questions*
> **un million de chiens**, *a million dogs*

▶ See p. 83.

■ After **quelque chose, rien, personne**, etc.:

> **quelque chose de beau**, *something beautiful*
> **rien de spécial**, *nothing special*

▶ See pp. 128 ff.

■ To join two nouns where the second is used adjectivally (the attributive noun):

> **la salle de bain**, *the bathroom*
> **la salle de séjour**, *the sitting room*

▶ For **de** with verbs see p. 55.
▶ For **de** used after adjectives, nouns, and adverbs see p. 51.

depuis, *since*

since (a place or a point in time)

> **tu n'as rien mangé depuis ton arrivée**, *you haven't eaten anything since your arrival* (*since you got here*)
> **c'est le premier péage depuis Lyon**, *it's the first toll point since Lyons*

for (a length of time)

> **elle regarde la télévision depuis une demi-heure**, *she's been watching television for half an hour*

▶ *For* with time may also be **pendant** or **pour**. See pp. 181, 182.
▶ For tenses with both the above meanings of **depuis** see pp. 17 and 21.

from (a place or a time), in **depuis ... jusqu'à**, *from ... to*

> **la côte méditerranéenne depuis Toulon jusqu'à Nice**, *the Mediterranean coast from Toulon to (as far as) Nice*

on est ouvert depuis huit heures du matin jusqu'à huit heures du soir, *we are open from eight in the morning until eight at night*

De … à is less emphatic:

du matin au soir, *from morning to night*

from (a place, = *out from*)

le panorama depuis le sommet est extraordinaire, *the panorama from the summit is remarkable*

dès, *as soon as*

as soon as; no later than (with future time)

je le ferai dès demain, *I'll do it no later than tomorrow*
dès son arrivée, *as soon as she gets here*
dès maintenant, *from now on*

as far back as; ever since (a point in past time onwards)

dès cette époque elle donnait des signes de folie, *even at that period (as far back as that period) she was showing signs of madness*

devant, *in front of*

▶ See **avant**, p. 170.

en, *in*

En expresses *in* in a more abstract or less specific way than does **dans**. It is always used without an article:

en ville, *in town*
en question, *in question*

except in a very few set expressions beginning with a vowel or 'mute' **h**:

en l'absence de, *in the absence of*
en l'air, *in the air*
en l'an ..., *in (the year)* ...
en l'honneur de, *in honour of*

in

en réponse à votre lettre, *in reply to your letter*
en forme de collier, *in the form of a necklace*
elle sortit en colère, *she went out angry* (*in anger*)
la cuisine était peinte en vert, *the kitchen was painted* (*in*) *green*
habillé en short, *dressed in shorts*

in (time: months, seasons, years)

en février, *in February*
en été, en automne et en hiver, *in summer, autumn, and winter* (but **au printemps**, *in spring*)
en 1999, *in 1999* (but **en l'an 1999**—note the article)

in, into (languages)

en français, *in French*
traduisez ça en anglais, *translate that into English*

in, to (with feminine singular names of countries and of continents)

on va en France, *we're going to France*
nous vivons en Europe, *we live in Europe*

▶ Otherwise *in* or *to* with countries is **au/aux**. See **à**, pp. 166, 167.

in (time within which)

je le ferai en deux minutes, *I'll do it* (*I'll have it done*) *in two minutes*

In (= *at the end of which time*) is **dans**:

> **je le ferai dans deux minutes**, *I'll do it* (*I'll start the job*) *in two minutes*

▶ See **dans**, p. 172.

as (= *in the shape of, as if it were*)

> **Monsieur Charles, en parfait gentleman, les accueillit très poliment**, *Charles, as the perfect gentleman, welcomed them very politely*
>
> **il me traite toujours en enfant**, *he always treats me as a child*
>
> **elle était déguisée en duchesse**, *she was dressed as a duchess*

by (with a form of transport, usually when one is 'in' the vehicle)

> **nous y allons en avion**, *we're going by plane*
>
> **ceux qui roulent en auto et en moto**, *those who travel by car and by motorbike* (also **à moto**)

▶ See also **à** (p. 167) and **par** (p. 180) with this meaning.

by, whilst, on (followed by the present participle)

> **je l'ai rencontrée en sortant du supermarché**, *I met her* (*whilst I was*) *coming out of the supermarket*

▶ See present participle, p. 35.

in the form of (English sometimes uses an attributive noun)

> **des chaussettes en accordéon**, *wrinkled socks* (*in the form of an accordion*)
>
> **un escalier en spirale**, *a spiral staircase* (*in the form of a spiral*)

made of (English often uses an attributive noun)

> **une table en acajou**, *a mahogany table*

De is also used with this meaning (see p. 174). **En** tends to draw more attention to the material of which the article is made than does **de**:

> **une montre en or,** *a gold watch*

on

> **j'ai un chat qui me suit en promenade,** *I've a cat that follows me on my walks*
> **on part en vacances,** *we're leaving on holiday*

entre, *between*

between (two people or things)

> **entre lui et moi,** *between him and me*
> **entre dix heures et minuit,** *between ten o'clock and midnight*

among(st) (more than two people or things)

> **ici vous êtes entre amis,** *here you are among friends*
> **les gens parlaient entre eux,** *people were talking among themselves*

Among(st) is, however, more frequently **parmi**:

> **parmi tous ceux qui étaient là, elle était la seule à bouger,** *amongst all those who were there she was the only one to move*

of (after **de** (**d'entre**) in expressions of quantity before pronouns)

> **quatre d'entre eux,** *four of them*
> **beaucoup d'entre vous,** *many of you*

envers, *towards* (figurative)

▶ See **vers,** p. 185.

hors (de), *except; out of*

▶ See **au-dehors de**, p. 168.

par, *by*

by

> **on commence par discuter, on finit par se
> quereller**, *you begin by discussing, you end by
> falling out*
> **par la D565**, *by the D565 road*
> **par ici/là**, (*by*) *this/that way*

by (with passive)

> **elle a été blessée par son mari**, *she was injured
> by her husband*

▶ See passive, p. 33.

by (with a few forms of transport, as an alternative to **en**)

> **par le train**, *by train*
> **par le métro**, *by underground*
> **par avion**, *by plane*

from (= *out of*, reason)

> **elle ne fait rien par conviction**, *she does nothing
> from (out of) conviction*

on, to

> **il était étendu par terre**, *he was lying on the
> ground*
> **elle est tombée par terre**, *she fell over; she fell to
> the ground* (from a standing position). Compare:
> **tomber à terre**, *fall to the ground* (from a height)

on, in (weather)

> **par un jour froid d'hiver**, *on a cold winter's day*
> **par un temps superbe**, *in splendid weather*

per, *a* (after numbers)

> **cinquante fois par semaine**, *fifty times a week*
> **deux par personne**, *two per person*

through

> **elle m'a vu par la fenêtre**, *she saw me through the window*
> **il a longtemps erré par les rues de Paris**, *for a long time he wandered through the streets of Paris*

Through where some difficulty is implied is **à travers**:

> **il se fraya un chemin à travers la foule**, *he battled his way through the crowd*

via

> **tu peux passer par Lyon ou par Dijon**, *you can go via Lyons or Dijon*

parmi, *among(st)*

▶ See **entre**, p. 179.

pendant, *during*

during

> **pendant ma visite**, *during my visit*

for (a completed period of time in the past)

> **ce mois-ci il a chômé pendant treize jours**, *this month he was out of work for thirteen days*

▶ See also **pour** (p. 182) and **depuis** (p. 175) meaning *for* with time.

pour, *for*

for (= *in favour of*)

> **tu votes pour les socialistes?**, *are you voting for the socialists?*
>
> **il faut peser le pour et le contre**, *you've got to weigh the pros and cons*

for (= *on behalf of*)

> **morts pour la France**, *they died for France*
>
> **elle y répondra pour toi**, *she'll reply to it for you*

for (intention)

> **ceci est pour toi**, *this is for you*
>
> **l'avion part pour Paris à trois heures cinq**, *the plane leaves for Paris at 3.05*

for (= *because of*)

> **on vous donne une contravention pour avoir laissé votre voiture devant le commissariat**, *you've been given a parking ticket for having left (for leaving) your car in front of the police station*

for (= *in exchange for*)

> **qu'est-ce que tu me donnes pour mon vélo?**, *what will you give me for my bike?*

for (plus intended length of time)

> **tu y vas pour trois mois?**, *you're going for three months?*

▶ See also **depuis** (p. 175) and **pendant** (p. 181) meaning *for* with time.

for (+ an amount)

> **tu en as là pour vingt minutes**, *you've enough work there for twenty minutes*

pour cent francs de sans-plomb, s'il vous plaît, *100 francs worth ('for 100 francs') of unleaded, please*

as for

pour ma part, je voudrais bien le faire, *as far as I'm concerned (as for me), I'd like to do it*

Quant à is also used in this sense:

quant à vous, *as for you*

per

dix pour cent, *ten per cent*

to (= in order to)

pour faire fonctionner la pompe, il faut d'abord sortir le robinet, *(in order) to operate the pump, the nozzle must first be withdrawn*

to (after **trop** + adjective, *too ...*, **assez** + adjective, *... enough*, and the verb **suffire**, *to be enough*)

tu es trop jeune pour y entrer, *you're too young to go in*

vous êtes assez informé pour savoir que ..., *you're well enough informed to know that ...*

cela suffira pour vous donner une idée de ce que nous pensons, *that will be enough to give you an idea of our thoughts*

quant à, *as for*

▶ See **pour**, above.

sous, *under*

under

ton hamster est sous ma chaise, *your hamster is under my chair*

Au-dessous de, *under*, implies *completely under* (=
underneath), or means *below* in figurative senses:

>> **les chiffres sont au-dessous de ce qu'on attendait**,
>> *the figures are below what we expected*

in

>> **tu ne peux pas sortir sous la pluie**, *you can't go
>> out in the rain*
>> **nous nous reverrons sous peu**, *we'll see each other
>> shortly (in a little while)*
>> **ils vécurent sous le règne de Louis XIV**, *they lived
>> in the reign of Louis XIV*

sur, *on*

on, on to

>> **je l'ai laissé sur le fauteuil**, *I left it on the armchair*
>> **monte sur l'échelle**, *climb up (on to) the ladder*
>> **elle était sur le point de m'interrompre**, *she was
>> about to interrupt me (on the point of interrupting
>> me)*
>> **assis sur le mur**, *sitting on the wall (on = hanging
>> on is* **à***. See p. 167)*
>> **sur notre droite**, *on our right*
>> **je n'ai pas d'argent sur moi**, *I haven't any money
>> on me*

by

>> **douze centimètres de haut sur dix centimètres de
>> large**, *12 cm. high by 10 cm. wide*

over

>> **son autorité sur vous est très restreinte**, *his
>> authority over you is very limited*
>> **le pont sur l'estuaire de la Seine**, *the bridge over
>> the Seine estuary*

▶ See also **au-dessus de**, *over*, p. 169.

in

> **j'ai laissé la clé sur la porte**, *I've left the key in the door*

in, out of

> **une personne sur dix**, *one person in ten*
> **dix-neuf sur vingt**, *19 out of 20*

upon

> **sur quoi, elle claqua la porte**, *whereupon (upon which) she slammed the door*

vers, *towards*

towards (place or point in time)

> **il s'en va vers la plage**, *he goes off towards the beach*
> **vers la fin de l'après-midi**, *towards the end of the afternoon*

Towards (figurative) is **envers**:

> **il est très bien intentionné envers nous**, *he is very well intentioned towards us*

about (with time of day)

> **vers dix heures et demie**, *about half past ten*

CROSS-REFERENCE LIST OF ENGLISH PREPOSITIONS

Prepositions presenting problems of translation are listed. These prepositions are cross-referenced to the list of French prepositions starting on p. 164. It is dangerous to take a French meaning from this list without subsequently checking its usage in the French list.

about
    = *concerning*, **de**, 173
    + time of day, **vers**, 185

according to
    d'après, 168

after
    place, **après**, 168
    time, **après**, 168

against
    contre, 171

among(st)
    chez, 171
    entre, 179
    parmi, 179

as
    = *in the shape of, as if it were*, **en**, 178

as far back as
    dès, 176

as for
    pour, 183

as soon as
    dès, 176

at
    numbers, **à**, 165
    place, **à**, 165
    time, **à**, 165

at X's (house, shop)
    chez, 171

above
    au-dessus de, 169
    par-dessus, 169

over
sur, 169; 184
au-dessus de, 169
par-dessus, 169

out of
sur, 185
hors de, 169

outside
au dehors de, 168
hors de, 169

per
par, 181
pour, 183

since
depuis, 175

than (+ quantity, in comparison)
de, 174

through
à travers, 181
par, 181

to
à, 167
after **trop/assez** + adj., **pour**, 183
after **suffire**, **pour**, 183
countries, feminine singular, **en**, 177
  masculine or plural, **à**, 167
de, 174
par, 180
= *in order to*, **pour**, 183

towards
figurative, **envers**, 185
place or point in time, **vers**, 185

| Conjunctions

■ Conjunctions are joining-words. They may join nouns or pronouns:

>**lui et son chien**, *he and his dog* (conjunction: **et**)

or phrases:

>**en arrivant ou en partant**, *on arriving or leaving* (conjunction: **ou**)

or clauses:

>**elle chante, mais elle ne joue pas**, *she sings but she doesn't play* (conjunction: **mais**)

■ They may also introduce a subordinate clause:

>**je le ferai quand j'aurai de l'argent**, *I'll do it when I have money* (conjunction: **quand**)

Many of the conjunctions that introduce subordinate clauses in French are two-word phrases with **que** as the second word:

>**je lui ai téléphoné pendant qu'elle travaillait**, *I phoned her whilst she was working* (conjunction: **pendant que**)

Quite often the first word of the phrase is a preposition with the same English meaning as the conjunction:

>**avant**, *before*, preposition
>**avant que**, *before*, conjunction

>**sans**, *without*, preposition
>**sans que**, *without*, conjunction

It is important to distinguish these—the preposition

will stand before a noun or (sometimes) the infinitive of a verb:

> **sans effort**, *without effort*
> **sans me regarder**, *without looking at me*

The conjunction will introduce a subordinate clause:

> **je l'organiserai avant qu'on leur parle**, *I'll organize it before anyone speaks to them*

▶ Many subordinating conjunctions are followed by the subjunctive. See p. 45.

■ The following conjunctions may give problems:

□ **aussi**, *so, therefore*

After **aussi**, verb and pronoun subject are inverted:

> **elle n'y montrait aucun intérêt, aussi est-il parti sans plus rien dire**, *she wasn't showing any interest, so he left without saying anything more*

Aussi can of course also be an adverb, meaning *also*.

□ **ni**, *nor*

After **sans**, **ni** is used where in English we should use *or*:

> **sans père ni mère**, *without father or mother*

□ **où**, *where*

After definite expressions of time **où** is used where in English we should use *when* or *that* or nothing at all:

> **l'instant où elle s'est retournée**, *the moment (when, that) she turned round*

See also **que** below.

□ **que**, *that*

Que becomes **qu'** before a vowel in written French. In spoken French it frequently remains as **que**.

After indefinite expressions of time **que** is used where in English we use *when*

> **un jour qu'il faisait beau**, *one day when it was fine*

See also **où** above.

Que is often used to avoid repeating a conjunction

> **quand tu viendras à Dijon et que tu verras la maison, tu seras enchanté**, *when you come to Dijon and (when you) see the house you'll be delighted*

When **que** replaces the conjunction **si** in this way it is followed by the subjunctive. See p. 48.

Que in comparisons means *than*

> **il est plus fort que moi**, *he's stronger than me*

▶ **Que** can also be a relative pronoun. See p. 112.

■ Paired conjunctions.

These conjunctions are used in much the same way as in English. The common ones are:

ni ... ni, *neither ... nor*
non seulement ... mais encore, *not only ... but also*
et ... et, *both ... and*
ou (bien) ... ou (bien), *either ... or (else)*
soit ... soit, *either ... or*

> **je n'ai ni argent ni ma carte Visa**, *I've neither money nor my Visa card*
> **non seulement lui mais encore toute sa famille sont venus déjeuner**, *not only he but all his family came to lunch*
> **on lui a pris et son agenda et son sac à main**, *they took both her diary and her handbag*
> **ou vous lui demandez pardon, ou je vous tue**, *either you apologize to her or I kill you*

on voyagera soit par le train soit par avion, *they'll travel either by train or by plane*

The last three pairs are used mostly in written French, a simple **et, ou,** or **ou bien** being used in the spoken language.

▶ For the use of **ne** with **ni ... ni** see p. 160.

Numbers, Time, Quantities

CARDINAL NUMBERS

The cardinal numbers are

0	zéro	24	vingt-quatre
1	un(e)	25	vingt-cinq
2	deux	26	vingt-six
3	trois	27	vingt-sept
4	quatre	28	vingt-huit
5	cinq	29	vingt-neuf
6	six	30	trente
7	sept	31	trente et un(e)
8	huit	32	trente-deux
9	neuf	40	quarante
10	dix	41	quarante et un(e)
11	onze	50	cinquante
12	douze	51	cinquante et un(e)
13	treize	60	soixante
14	quatorze	61	soixante et un(e)
15	quinze	70	soixante-dix
16	seize	71	soixante et onze
17	dix-sept	72	soixante-douze
18	dix-huit	80	quatre vingts
19	dix-neuf	81	quatre-vingt-un(e)
20	vingt	82	quatre-vingt-deux
21	vingt et un(e)	90	quatre-vingt-dix
22	vingt-deux	91	quatre-vingt-onze
23	vingt-trois	92	quatre-vingt-douze

100	cent	2 000	deux mille
101	cent un(e)	1 000 000	un million
200	deux cents	1 000 200	un million deux
201	deux cent un(e)		cents
1 000	mille	2 000 000	deux millions
1 001	mille un(e)	1 000 000 000	un milliard
1 002	mille deux	2 000 000 000	deux milliards

Thousands and millions are written with spaces (formerly sometimes with full stops) rather than, as in English, with commas. The comma is used for a decimal point—see p. 215.

■ There is no **-s** on the plural of **vingt** and **cent** when these are followed by another number.

■ There is never an **-s** on the plural of **mille** meaning *thousands*. **Le mille**, meaning *mile*, takes a plural **-s**.

■ **Million** and **milliard** are nouns. With a noun immediately following, they take **de**:

> **un million de soldats**, *a million soldiers*

but

> **un million deux cent mille soldats**, *1,200,000 soldiers*

All other numbers are adjectives. They are invariable, except that those ending in **un** agree with a following feminine noun (changing to **une**).

■ There is no **un** before **cent**, **mille**, meaning *one hundred*, *one thousand*:

> **mille francs**, *one thousand francs*

There is no **et** after **cent** or **mille**:

> **cent douze**, *a hundred and twelve*
> **mille un**, *one thousand and one*

except in the book title, *Les mille et une nuits*, *A Thousand and One Nights*.

■ Figures are grouped in twos when you speak telephone numbers:

> 33 56 08 = **trente-trois cinquante-six zéro huit**
> 445 35 71 = **quatre cent quarante-cinq trente-cinq soixante et onze**

■ In Belgium, Switzerland, and Canada **septante**, **octante** or **huitante**, and **nonante** are used for 70, 80, and 90.

■ The numbers **six** and **dix** have each three different pronunciations. Before a consonant the **-x** is not pronounced; before a vowel or **h** 'mute' it is pronounced **z**; where **six** and **dix** stand after the noun (**chapitre six**) or alone (**le dix**) the **-x** is pronounced **s**.

The final consonants of **cinq**, **huit**, and (usually) **neuf** are not pronounced before another consonant, except in dates.

The **f** of **neuf** is pronounced **v** before the words **ans**, *years*, and **heures**, *o'clock*; before other words beginning with a vowel or **h** 'mute' it is pronounced **f**.

The **t** of **vingt** is usually pronounced in the numbers 21–29; it is not pronounced in dates: **le vin[gt] août**.

■ Before **huit** and **onze**, **le** does not become **l'**:

> **tu as le huit de trèfle?**, *do you have the eight of clubs?*
> **le onze juin**, *the eleventh of June*

This also applies to the ordinal forms:

> **le huitième**, *the eighth*
> **le onzième**, *the eleventh*

ORDINAL NUMBERS

Ordinal numbers (*first*, *second*, *third*, etc.) are formed by removing the final **-e** of the cardinal number (if it ends in **-e**) and adding **-ième**:

8, **huit** → 8th, **huitième**
12, **douze** → 12th, **douzième**
21, **vingt et un** → 21st, **vingt et unième**

Exceptions:

premier (fem: **première**), 1st
cinquième, 5th
neuvième, 9th

> **la première fois**, *the first time* (but **la trente et
> unième fois**, *the thirty-first time*)
> **le cinquième article**, *the fifth article*
> **le vingt-neuvième livre**, *the twenty-ninth book*

■ **Second** (fem: **seconde**) is an alternative to
deuxième, mainly used where there is no reference to a
third or subsequent thing or person. Notice though:

> **je suis en seconde**, *I'm in the fifth form* (French
> secondary schools count their classes in the
> opposite order to English schools)

■ Ordinals may be abbreviated thus 1er, 2e, 3e, etc., or
1°, 2°, 3°, etc. The latter is short for the Latin *primo,
secundo, tertio,* etc.

■ When cardinal and ordinal numbers are used together
the order is the reverse of that in English:

> **les cinq premiers mois**, *the first five months*

■ French uses cardinal numbers where we use ordinal
numbers for days of the month and numbers of kings:

> **le vingt mai**, *the twentieth of May*
> **Henri quatre**, *Henri the Fourth*

However, for *first* French uses **premier**:

> **le premier septembre**, *the first of September*
> **Charles premier**, *Charles the First*

French, like English, uses cardinals for act, scene,

volume, and chapter numbers, but in all these cases uses **premier** for *one*:

> **acte premier**, *act one*
> **acte deux**, *act two*
> **chapitre premier**, *chapter one*

APPROXIMATE NUMBERS

Approximate numbers are formed in French by adding **-aine** to the cardinal number (the final **-e**, if any, is first dropped). They can only be based on 8, 15, tens up to 60, and 100. The resultant number is a feminine noun and is followed by **de**:

> **une quinzaine de francs**, *about fifteen francs*
> **une vingtaine de personnes**, *about twenty (a score of) people*
> **une cinquantaine de cahiers**, *about fifty exercise books*

■ **Mille**, *thousand*, forms **un millier**:

> **un millier de bateaux**, *about a thousand boats*

■ These nouns can be used in the plural:

> **des centaines de voitures**, *hundreds of cars*

■ **Une douzaine**, *a dozen*, though precise, is formed in the same way as the approximate numbers:

> **une douzaine d'œufs**, *a dozen eggs*

Une quinzaine can also be used precisely to mean *a fortnight*, and **une huitaine** is sometimes found as an alternative to **une semaine**, *a week*.

FRACTIONS

Ordinal numbers are used to express fractions, as in English:

$^1/_5$ = **un cinquième**
$^3/_8$ = **trois huitièmes**

Exceptions:

un quart = $^1/_4$, **trois quarts** = $^3/_4$
un tiers = $^1/_3$, **deux tiers** = $^2/_3$
un demi = $^1/_2$

■ *Half* as a mathematical term is **le demi**:

les deux demis, *the two halves*

but in ordinary language, *half of* something is **la moitié de**:

la moitié du temps il ne fait rien, *half the time he does nothing*

Half as an adjective is **demi**. It is hyphenated to the noun and is invariable:

une demi-journée, *a half day*
une demi-heure, *a half hour* (but **un quart d'heure**, *quarter of an hour*)

La demie is *the half-hour*:

la demie sonne, *it's striking half past*

■ Decimals are expressed in French with a comma:

$1\cdot5 \rightarrow$ **1,5 (un virgule cinq)**

■ The main mathematical signs are:

+ **plus**	÷ **divisé par**
− **moins**	^{2} **au carré**
× **fois**	% **pour cent**

trois plus deux égalent cinq, *three plus two equals five*
dix au carré, *ten squared*
onze pour cent, *eleven per cent*

TIME AND DATE

Time of day

Quelle heure est-il?, *what time is it?*
Avez-vous l'heure, monsieur/madame? (politer!)

Il est:

> **une heure,** *one o'clock*
> **une heure cinq,** *five past one*
> **deux heures,** *two o'clock*
> **deux heures et** (or **un**) **quart,** *quarter past two*
> **trois heures et demie, trois heures trente,** *half past three*
> **quatre heures moins le** (or **moins un**) **quart,** *quarter to four*
> **cinq heures moins une (minute),** *a minute to five*
> **midi,** *noon*
> **midi et demi, midi trente,** *half past twelve*
> **minuit,** *midnight*
> **minuit et demi, minuit trente,** *half past twelve*

■ **Heure(s)** is used where English uses *o'clock*. **Et demie** is used after hours, **et demi** after **midi, minuit**. With quarters the article **le** is used after **moins** but not after **et**.

■ The forms **trois heures trente,** etc. are adopted from the twenty-four hour clock, used in timetables and all official documents. This follows the pattern:

> **une heure dix, 01h10**
> **douze heures quarante-cinq, 12h45**
> **dix-neuf heures cinquante-cinq, 19h55**

■ French has no equivalents to *a.m.* and *p.m.* Where necessary, **du matin,** *in the morning,* **de l'après-midi,** *in the afternoon,* or **du soir,** *in the evening,* are added as appropriate:

trois heures du matin, *3 a.m.*

■ *In the morning* (*afternoon, evening*) is simply **le matin** (**l'après-midi, le soir**). *At night* is **la nuit.** *Every morning* (etc.) is **tous les matins.**

Prepositions etc. with times of day

à, *at, by*

> **alors, on se revoit à trois heures précises,** *right, we'll meet at three o'clock sharp*
> **on sera là à midi,** *we'll be there by twelve*

à partir de, *from*

> **je serai au bureau à partir de neuf heures et demie,** *I shall be in the office from 9.30*

au bout de, *after*

> **au bout d'un petit instant elle recommença,** *after a moment she began again*

de ... à, *from ... to*

> **le restaurant est ouvert de midi à deux heures et demie,** *the restaurant is open from 12 to 2.30*

environ, *about*

> **il est environ sept heures** (or **sept heures environ**), *it's about seven o'clock*

jusqu'à, *until*

> **jusqu'à quatre heures de l'après-midi,** *until 4 p.m.*

pas plus tard que, *no later than*

> **il faut y arriver pas plus tard que deux heures et demie,** *you must get there no later than half past two*

passé, *past*

> **il est huit heures passées,** *it's past eight o'clock*

vers, *about*

> **il est parti vers les cinq heures,** *he left about five*

Days, months, seasons

days of the week	*months of the year*
dimanche, *Sunday*	**janvier,** *January*
lundi, *Monday*	**février,** *February*
mardi, *Tuesday*	**mars,** *March*
mercredi, *Wednesday*	**avril,** *April*
jeudi, *Thursday*	**mai,** *May*
vendredi, *Friday*	**juin,** *June*
samedi, *Saturday*	**juillet,** *July*
	août, *August*
today, etc.	**septembre,** *September*
avant-hier, *the day before yesterday*	**octobre,** *October*
hier, *yesterday*	**novembre,** *November*
aujourd'hui, *today*	**décembre,** *December*
demain, *tomorrow*	
après-demain, *the day after tomorrow*	*seasons*
	le printemps, *spring*
la veille, *the day before*	**l'été,** *summer*
le lendemain, *the day after*	**l'automne,** *autumn*
	l'hiver, *winter*

Days, months, and seasons are all masculine and are spelt with a small letter.

Parts of the day

hier, *yesterday*
ce (cet), *this*
demain, *tomorrow*
dimanche, *Sunday* (etc.)
le lendemain, *the day after, in the ...*

{ **matin,** *morning*
après-midi, *afternoon*
soir, *evening*

on vous verra dimanche soir, *we'll see you Sunday evening*

cela est arrivé ce matin, *that happened this morning*

on s'est brouillés le lendemain soir, *we quarrelled the following evening*

The evening before is **la veille au soir**.

Cette nuit means either *tonight* or *last night*, according to context:

tu dormiras bien cette nuit!, *you'll sleep well tonight!*

je n'ai pas dormi cette nuit, *I didn't sleep last night*

Prepositions with days, months, seasons, etc.

■ *In* with months is **en** or **au mois de**:

en avril, *in April*

au mois d'août, *in August*

■ *In* with seasons is **en**, except **le printemps**:

en hiver, *in winter*

au printemps, *in spring*

■ *In* with years is **en** or **en l'an**. **Mil** is used instead of **mille** in writing years:

en l'an mil neuf cent quarante-cinq, *in 1945*

In spoken French **dix-neuf** (etc.) is very often used for **mil neuf** (etc.):

en seize cent douze, *in 1612*

In the eighties (etc.) is **dans les années quatre-vingt** (note spelling here: no **-s**, hyphen).

■ *In* with centuries is **au**:

> **au vingtième siècle**, *in the twentieth century*

■ *On* with days in the plural is **le**:

> **il ne travaille que le mercredi**, *he only works on Wednesdays*

■ *On* with days in the singular is not translated:

> **elle arrive mercredi**, *she's coming on Wednesday*
> **elle arrive mercredi matin**, *she's coming on Wednesday morning*

The date

The date is expressed with **le**, plus a cardinal number (except for **premier**, *first*), plus the month. *On* before a date is not translated:

> **on sera à Paris le quatorze juillet**, *we are going to be in Paris on the fourteenth of July*
> **nous sommes le premier juin**, *today's the first of June*

When the day is expressed, the article before the date is usually dropped:

> **lundi, vingt mai** or **le lundi vingt mai**, *Monday the twentieth of May*

MEASUREMENT

Length, breadth, height

Quelle est $\left\{ \begin{array}{l} \textbf{la longueur} \\ \textbf{la largeur} \\ \textbf{la hauteur} \end{array} \right\}$ **de cette pièce?**,

How $\left\{ \begin{array}{l} long \\ wide \\ high \end{array} \right\}$ *is this room?*

— **Elle a trois mètres dix de** $\left\{\begin{array}{l}\textbf{long}\\\textbf{large}\\\textbf{haut}\end{array}\right\}$, *It's*

    3.10 metres $\left\{\begin{array}{l}long\\wide\\high\end{array}\right\}$

■ **Faire** can be used instead of **avoir**:

> **elle fait trois mètres de long**, *it's three metres long*

■ *By* in measurements is **sur**:

> **cette pièce fait trois mètres sur quatre**, *this room is three metres by four*

Other common ways of expressing dimension

■ **Long** (etc.) **de**:

> **cette poutre est longue de trois mètres**, *this beam is three metres long*
> **une poutre longue de trois mètres**, *a beam three metres long*

■ **De longueur** (etc.):

> **cette poutre a trois mètres de longueur**, *this beam is three metres long*
> **une poutre de trois mètres de longueur**, *a beam three metres long*

■ **D'une longueur** (etc.) **de**:

> **cette poutre est d'une longueur de trois mètres**, *this beam is three metres long*
> **une poutre d'une longueur de trois mètres**, *a beam three metres long*

The same constructions can be used with **profond/la profondeur**, *deep/depth,* and **épais/l'épaisseur**, *thick/*

thickness, except the **de long** construction, which cannot be used with **épais** and **profond**.

Personal measurements

Quelle taille faites-vous?, *What size are you?*

Combien mesurez-vous?, *What is your height?*

Quel est votre tour de $\begin{Bmatrix} \textbf{poitrine} \\ \textbf{taille} \\ \textbf{hanches} \end{Bmatrix}$**?**, *What is your* $\begin{Bmatrix} bust \\ waist \\ hip \end{Bmatrix}$ *size?*

Quelle pointure chaussez-vous/faites-vous?, *What is your shoe size?*

Notice the three meanings of **la taille**: *size, height, waist*. Only the context makes clear which is meant.

Word Order

Special cases (after direct speech; after **peut-être**, **à peine**, **aussi**; in exclamations; after **dont**) *210*
Word order in direct questions *211*
Word order in indirect questions *213*

Word order in French is generally the same as in English, except that:

■ Adjectives usually follow their nouns. See p. 138.

■ Object pronouns precede the verb. See p. 105.

■ Adverbs follow the verb. See p. 156.

■ Negatives stand in two parts around the verb. See p. 159.

■ The 'strong' position in the French sentence is at the end, so where there are, for instance, two or more adverb phrases, the more important one goes to the end. Thus the answer to **quand l'as-tu retrouvé?** (*when did you find it?*) might be:

> **je l'ai retrouvé dans la voiture hier soir**, *I found it last night in the car*

English usage varies, but the more important phrase tends to come first in English, straight after the verb, as in the above example.

■ Word order in direct and indirect questions is treated on pp. 211 and 213.

SPECIAL CASES

■ After direct speech, subject and 'saying' verb are inverted:

> **«Bonjour, dit-il, ça va?»**, *'Hello,' he said, 'How are you?'*
>
> **«Vraiment?» répondit l'agent**, *'Really?' the policeman replied*

Notice what happens in compound tenses:

> **«Bonjour, a-t-il dit, ça va?»**, *'Hello,' he said, 'How are you?'*
>
> **«Vraiment?» a répondu l'agent**, *'Really?' the policeman replied*

Although the pronoun inversion is like the question form (**a-t-il dit?**) the noun inversion is not (**l'agent a-t-il répondu?**).

■ In a clause beginning **peut-être**, *perhaps*, **à peine**, *scarcely*, or **aussi**, *therefore*, verb and subject pronoun are inverted:

> **peut-être a-t-elle froid**, *perhaps she's cold*
>
> **à peine son père était-il arrivé que le repas commença**, *his father had scarcely got there when the meal began*
>
> **maintenant tu me dis la vérité, aussi suis-je content**, *now you're telling me the truth, so I'm happy*

This inversion is literary, however. In everyday French it is avoided: **peut-être** would be placed after the verb, or the sentence would begin with **peut-être que**:

> **elle a peut-être froid**
>
> **peut-être qu'elle a froid**

A peine would similarly be placed after the verb, and **donc** would be substituted for **aussi**:

> son père était à peine arrivé que le repas commença
>
> maintenant tu me dis la vérité, donc je suis content

■ In exclamations after **comme** and **que** French has normal word order where English does not:

> **comme il est beau!**, *how handsome he is!*
> **que tu es bête!**, *how silly you are!*

■ After **dont** French always has normal word order where English sometimes does not:

> **le médecin dont tu connais la fille**, *the doctor whose daughter you know*
> **le médecin dont la fille est malade**, *the doctor whose daughter is ill*

▶ See also p. 115.

WORD ORDER IN DIRECT QUESTIONS

Simple questions

Simple questions are formed:

■ By a statement with an interrogative (rising) intonation. This is the commonest way to form a question in speech:

> **c'est une Française?**, *is she French?*

■ By prefixing **est-ce que** to the statement. This is also common in both speech and writing:

> **est-ce que vous prenez du sucre?**, *do you take sugar?*

■ By inverting verb and subject pronoun and putting a hyphen between them:

> **prenez-vous du café?**, *will you have some coffee?*

An extra **-t** is inserted where the verb ends in **-e** or **-a**:

> **a-t-il déjà dîné?**, *has he already eaten?*

In modern French there is, for most verbs, no inverted form of the interrogative with the **je** form of the present tense. **Est-ce que** or a simple question intonation is used.

Inversion is, however, still used with the **je** form of the present tense of **pouvoir**, **devoir**, **être**, and, occasionally, **avoir**:

> **puis-je vous revoir?**, *may I see you again?* (NB never '**peux-je**')
> **que dois-je dire?**, *what am I to say?*
> **suis-je encore de tes amis?**, *am I still one of your friends?*
> **ai-je tout corrigé?**, *have I marked everything?*

■ By stating the noun subject and then asking the question about it using a pronoun. This produces the sequence noun, verb, hyphen, pronoun:

> **votre chien est-il toujours malade?**, *is your dog still ill?*

This construction is literary and is hardly ever found in everyday French.

Questions following question words (interrogative adverbs)

Questions following words such as **pourquoi**, *why*, **quand**, *when*, **où**, *where*, etc. are formed:

■ With a statement pronounced with an interrogative (rising) intonation, following the question word:

où tu vas?, *where are you going?*

This construction is frowned upon in the written language but is extremely common in spoken French.

■ With the question word followed by **est-ce que** and a statement:

où est-ce que tu vas?, *where are you going?*

This is common in both written and spoken French.

■ With the question word followed by the verb, a hyphen and the subject pronoun:

comment as-tu fait cela?, *how did you do that?*

■ With the question word followed by the verb and the subject noun:

quand part le train de Marseille?, *when does the Marseilles train go?*

This form is not possible after **pourquoi** and often sounds clumsy in compound tenses. In these cases one of the other forms is used.

■ With the question word followed by the noun subject, the question then being asked about this using a pronoun:

pourquoi le train de Marseille part-il de cette voie?, *why does the Marseilles train leave from this platform?*

This construction is literary and is hardly ever found in everyday French.

▶ For questions introduced by the interrogative pronouns **qui, que**, etc. (*who, what*), see p. 119.

WORD ORDER IN INDIRECT QUESTIONS

An indirect question is one that is reported in some way (direct question: *why is he there?*, indirect question:

I don't know why he's there). As in English the word
order is: question word followed by normal order:

> **je ne sais pas pourquoi il est là**, *I don't know why
> he's there*

If the subject of the indirect question is a noun and the
verb would otherwise end the sentence, verb and noun
are inverted:

> **je me demande si ta copine est là**, *I wonder if
> your friend is there*
> **je me demande où est ta copine**, *I wonder where
> your friend is*

In this way French avoids leaving a weak word like **est**
in the strong position at the end of the sentence.

Punctuation

French punctuation is largely similar to English, with the following exceptions:

COMMAS

■ Commas are not used in writing large numbers in French. Where we would put a comma, modern French leaves a gap:

> English: 44,000,000   French: 44 000 000

■ Commas are used in decimals where we would use a decimal point or a full stop:

> English: 3·25 or 3.25   French: 3,25

CAPITAL LETTERS

Capitals are used much less frequently in French than in English. French uses small letters for:

■ Country adjectives:

> **il a l'air italien**, *he looks Italian*
> **une assiette anglaise**, *a plate of cold meats*

■ Language nouns:

> **elle parle français**, *she speaks French*

but not nouns of nationality:

> **c'est une Française**, *she's French*

■ Personal and professional titles, ranks:

> **monsieur Dubois** (but **M. Dubois**)
> **le docteur Artin**
> **le général Leclerc**

■ Street, square, avenue, etc., in names:

> **tu descends place de la Concorde**, *you get out at
> the Place de la Concorde*
> **la mer Méditerranée**, *the Mediterranean Sea*
> **elle demeure boulevard Raspail**, *she lives in the
> Boulevard Raspail*
> **7, rue Victor-Hugo**

■ Points of the compass:

> **le sud**, *the south*; **le nord**, *the north* (but **le Nord**,
> name of the region)

■ Names of days, months:

> **dimanche prochain**, *next Sunday*
> **en janvier dernier**, *last January*

■ Cheeses and wines named after places:

> **le camembert**, *Camembert*
> **le beaujolais**, *Beaujolais*

■ Quite often after an exclamation mark where the sense
is not complete. There are two examples in the Daudet
extract on p. 218 (in the section on inverted commas).

COLON AND DASH

Colon

The colon is used more frequently than in English.
As well as being used as a long pause, intermediate

between a semi-colon and a full stop (as in English), the colon is used where an amplification or explanation is to follow next. English often uses a dash for this, French hardly ever:

> **La seule solution: refaire le toit**, *The only solution—repair the roof*

Dash

■ Used at the beginning and end of parentheses, as in English:

> **Le patron parlait — il aimait beaucoup parler — et en même temps il tapait sur la table**, *The boss was speaking—he was very fond of speaking—and at the same time he was tapping on the table*

■ Used to mark off items in a list:

> **il sera nécessaire de**
> **— remplacer les poutres**
> **— refaire le toit**
> **— réparer les rebords des fenêtres**
> **— reconstruire les placards**
>
> *It will be necessary to*
> *replace the beams,*
> *redo the roof,*
> *repair the window-sills,*
> *remake the cupboards*

■ Used to indicate a change of speaker in direct speech (see below, inverted commas).

SUSPENSION POINTS (...)

These may indicate that the sentence breaks off, as in English. In French, they may also indicate that what is to come next is comic, incongruous, or unexpected. English often uses a dash here:

> **45 milliards de francs par mois ... la moitié du budget de l'État!**, *45 billion francs a year—half the national budget!*

INVERTED COMMAS

These are printed « » or " ". Single inverted commas ' ', are almost never used in French.

Inverted commas are placed at the beginning and end of a section of dialogue. Within that dialogue change of speaker is indicated by a new paragraph beginning with a dash (—), but the inverted commas are not closed or reopened. Short phrases indicating who is speaking, together with any adverbial qualifications, (e.g., **répondit-il d'un air distrait**) are included within the dialogue without closing or reopening the inverted commas. Longer interpolations (of at least one complete sentence) do entail closing and reopening the inverted commas.

The following extract from Daudet's *Lettres de mon moulin* illustrates all these points:

> **«C'est fini ... Je n'en fais plus.**
>
> **— Qu'est-ce qu'il y a donc, père Gaucher? demanda le prieur, qui se doutait bien un peu de ce qu'il y avait.**
>
> **— Ce qu'il y a, monseigneur? ... Il y a que je bois, que je bois comme un misérable ...**
>
> **— Mais je vous avais dit de compter vos gouttes.**
>
> **— Ah, bien oui! compter mes gouttes! c'est par gobelets qu'il faudrait compter maintenant ... Que le feu de Dieu me brûle si je m'en mêle encore!»**

C'est le chapitre qui ne riait plus.
«Mais, malheureux, vous nous ruinez! criait
l'argentier en agitant son grand-livre.
— Préférez-vous que je me damne?»

'It's over. I'm not making any more.'

'What's the matter then, *père Gaucher?*' asked
the prior, who rather suspected what the matter
was.

'What's the matter, *monseigneur?* The matter is,
I'm drinking, drinking like a scoundrel.'

'But I told you to count your sips.'

'Oh yes, count my sips! It's cupfuls I'd have to
be counting now. May the fire of God consume me
if I have anything more to do with it!'

Now it was the chapter who were no longer
laughing.

'But, you wretched man, you're ruining us!'
cried the treasurer, waving his ledger.

'Would you rather I damned myself?'

Translation Problems

The following list is alphabetical. It includes items not covered in the body of the grammar, or treated in a number of different places and more conveniently brought together here. Translation problems not covered here should be tackled via the index, or, in the case of prepositions, the alphabetical lists on pp. 185 (English) and 164 (French).

-ING

The *-ing* form of the verb is basically the present participle, but it has other uses in English, few of which correspond to the French.

■ *-ing* as adjective (the *-ing* word stands in front of a noun):

> *the setting sun*
> *the deciding factor*

In this case the French word will also be an adjective. It may be a present participle used as an adjective, as in English:

> **le soleil couchant**, *the setting sun* (**se coucher**, *set* →present participle **couchant**)

or it may be an ordinary adjective:

> **le facteur décisif**, *the deciding factor*

► See present participle, p. 34.

■ *-ing* as a verb in a phrase:

> *he spoke, looking at me closely*
> *getting off the bus, I saw Micheline*

In this case the *-ing* word is translated by a present participle, usually preceded by **en**, *whilst*:

> **il parla, en me regardant de près**, *he spoke, looking at me closely*
> **en descendant de l'autobus, j'ai vu Micheline**, *getting off the bus, I saw Micheline*

This construction can only be used where both verbs have the same subject (*he* spoke and *he* looked at me, *I* got off and *I* saw her). Where the subjects are different, **qui** (or alternatively, after verbs of perception only, an infinitive) has to be used:

> **j'ai vu Micheline qui descendait de l'autobus**, or
> **j'ai vu Micheline descendre de l'autobus**, *I saw Micheline getting off the bus*

In this case the subjects are different (*I* saw, but *Micheline* got off).

► For more detail see p. 35.

■ *-ing* after a preposition:

> *without stopping*
> *before eating*

This is an infinitive:

> **sans parler**, *without speaking*
> **avant de manger**, *before eating*

With some prepositions, notably **après**, *after*, the sense may demand a perfect infinitive:

> **après avoir mangé**, *after eating*
> **après être sorti**, *after going out*

After the preposition **en**, *whilst, by, in*, a present participle is used:

> **en tournant**, *whilst turning*

▶ For more detail see pp. 52 (infinitives after prepositions) and 53 (perfect infinitive).

■ *-ing* in 'continuous' tenses: *I am running, I was running, I shall be running, I have been running*, etc.

French does not use a present participle for these: *I run* and *I am running* are the same in French: **je cours**, *I have been running* and *I have run* are the same, **j'ai couru**. Only in the case of the imperfect does a special 'continuous' tense exist: **je courais**, *I was running*.

If the continuous nature of an action needs to be emphasized (which is not usually the case), **être en train de** is used:

> **je serai en train de déjeuner**, *I shall be eating my lunch*

▶ For more details see p. 16.

Superficially similar to the above are sentences such as 'she was leaning on the fence', 'he was lying on the ground'. In this case, however, French views *lying*, *leaning*, etc. as adjectives and uses **être** plus a past participle:

> **elle était accoudée sur la clôture**, *she was leaning on the fence*
> **il était couché par terre**, *he was lying on the ground*

▶ For further details see p. 39.

■ *-ing* after a verb:

> *he begins typing*
> *she stops telephoning*
> *they love swimming*

This is an infinitive in French, preceded by the preposition appropriate to the main verb:

> **il commence à taper à la machine**, *he begins typing*
> **elle s'arrête de téléphoner**, *she stops telephoning*
> **ils adorent nager**, *they love swimming*

■ *-ing* after a verb with an object:

> *he stops her telephoning*
> *she heard him laughing*

This is also an infinitive in French, preceded by the preposition appropriate to the main verb:

> **il l'empêche de téléphoner**, *he stops her telephoning*
> **elle l'a entendu rire**, *she heard him laughing*

▶ For the prepositions that verbs take before an infinitive see p. 51.

■ *-ing* as subject of the sentence (the verbal noun):

> *walking tires me*
> *telephoning is easier*

This is an infinitive in French:

> **me promener me fatigue**, *walking tires me*
> **téléphoner est plus simple**, *telephoning is easier*

However, French prefers to avoid this use of the infinitive at the beginning of the sentence, and usually makes the infinitive depend on the other verb:

> **ça me fatigue de me promener**, *it tires me to walk*
> **c'est plus simple de téléphoner**, *it's easier to telephone*

▶ See also the infinitive as verbal noun, p. 50.

■ *-ing* as a noun

English uses *-ing* nouns for many sorts of activity and sports. These are translated by other nouns in French:

> *fishing*, **la pêche**
> *swimming*, **la natation**
> *singing*, **le chant**
> *horse-riding*, **l'équitation**

IT IS

It is with nouns and adjectives

■ Where *it is* refers to a noun that has already been mentioned, it is translated by **il est** or **elle est** according to the gender of that noun:

> **la clé? Elle est sur la porte**, *the key? It's in the door*
> **ma nouvelle robe, ah oui, elle est bleue**, *my new dress, yes, it's blue*

■ Where *it is* introduces a noun or pronoun, it is translated by **c'est**, whatever the gender of the noun or pronoun. The plural (*those are*) is **ce sont**:

> **c'est une Citroën**, *it's a Citroën*
> **c'est moi!**, *it's me!*
> **ce sont des mouettes**, *those are seagulls*

C'est is similarly used to introduce adverbial expressions:

> **c'est à Noël qu'elle vient**, *it's at Christmas that she's coming*

■ Where *it is* refers back to something other than a noun (a noun clause, a previous sentence, etc.), **c'est** is used.

> **il parle italien? Oui, c'est possible**, *he speaks Italian? Yes, it's possible*

■ Where *it is* introduces an adjective followed by **que** or **de**, **il est** is used:

> **il est possible qu'il parle italien**, *it's possible that he speaks Italian*
> **il est difficile de traduire cela**, *it's difficult to translate that*

However, in the spoken language **c'est** is very often used in this case too:

> **c'est possible qu'il parle Italien**, *it's possible he speaks Italian*

■ In all cases except the last **cela est** may be used instead of **c'est**:

> **cela est possible**, *it's (that's) possible*

It is, with weather, time, etc.

■ *It* is **il** with:

☐ Weather verbs, both simple verbs

> **il pleut**, *it's raining*
> **il neige**, *it's snowing*

and those constructed with **faire**

> **il fait du vent**, *it's windy*
> **il fait beau**, *it's fine*

☐ Time of day

> **il est cinq heures**, *it's five o'clock*
> **il est midi et demi**, *it's half past twelve*

☐ The time expressions: **tard**, *late*, **tôt**, *early*, **temps**, *time*

> **il est tard**, *it's late*
> **il est temps de partir**, *it's time to go*
> **il est temps que tu partes**, *it's time you went*

■ With other time expressions **c'est** is used:

> **c'est dimanche**, *it's Sunday*
> **c'est janvier**, *it's January*
> **c'est le printemps**, *it's spring*
> **c'est le 18 mai**, *it's the 18th of May*

■ **Pouvoir**, *can*, and **devoir**, *ought to*, *should*, may be introduced into these constructions:

> **ce doit être possible**, *it ought to be possible*
> **il peut neiger**, *it may snow*

▶ For further details see impersonal verbs, pp. 74 ff.

JUST (adverb)

■ *just = exactly*: **juste**; **justement**

> **tu as juste trois minutes**, *you have just three minutes*
> **c'est juste au-dessus de la porte**, *it's just above the door*
> **on a sonné juste au moment où je me mettais dans le bain**, *someone rang the bell just when I was getting into the bath*
> **c'est justement ce que je dis toujours**, *that's just what I always say*

■ *just = only*: **seul; seulement**

    un seul, *just one*
    seulement deux, trois, etc., *just two, three*, etc.
    une seule fois, *just once*

■ *just* in *have/had just*: **venir de** + infinitive

    je viens de le faire, *I've just done it*
    on venait de l'ouvrir, *they had just opened it*

▶ See pp. 18 and 21 for more details on tenses with **venir de**.

■ *just* in *just as* (= *equally*): **tout**

    cela est tout aussi difficile, *that's just as difficult*

■ *just* with a following verb: **ne faire que** + infinitive

    elle n'a fait que pleurer, *she just cried*

-SELF

■ *-self* as direct or indirect object: reflexive pronoun (**me, te, se,** etc.) before verb:

    il s'est distingué, *he distinguished himself*
    je me disais la même chose, *I was saying the same thing to myself*

▶ For further details see reflexive pronouns, p. 30.

■ *-self* as a strengthener of the subject: disjunctive pronoun + **-même** (**moi-même, toi-même,** etc.) placed after verb:

    tu l'as fait toi-même?, *you did it yourself?*

▶ For further details see disjunctive pronouns, p. 109 and disjunctives with **-même**, p. 111.

■ *-self* after preposition: disjunctive pronoun (**moi, toi,** etc.) with or without **-même**:

> **je ne parle que pour moi**, *I can only speak for myself*
>
> **il n'écrit que pour lui-même**, *he writes only for himself*

■ *oneself* is **soi(-même)**:

> **on ne peut pas le garder pour soi(-même)**, *one can't keep it for oneself*

▶ For further details on the use of **soi** see p. 109.

SINCE

■ Preposition: **depuis**

> **je t'attends depuis deux heures et demie**, *I've been waiting for you since half past two*
>
> **je t'attendais depuis deux heures et demie**, *I had been waiting for you since half past two*

The tenses with **depuis** are different from the English ones in positive statements: *have been ... ing* = French present, *had been ... ing* = French imperfect. With a negative the tense is the same as in English:

> **je ne l'ai pas vue depuis la boum**, *I haven't seen her since the party*

▶ **Depuis** can also mean *for*. For more details on tenses with **depuis** see pp. 17 and 21.

■ Adverb: **depuis**

> **tu l'a vue depuis?**, *have you seen her since?*

The adverb **depuis** does not affect the tense of the verb.

■ Time conjunction: **depuis que**

> **elle travaille depuis que son mari est mort**, *she has been working (has worked) ever since her husband died*
>
> **elle allait à pied depuis que la voiture avait fini par tomber en panne**, *she had been walking (ever) since the car had finally broken down*
>
> **je ne dors plus depuis qu'il est de retour**, *I'm not sleeping any more since he's back*

Tenses with **depuis que**, conjunction, are the same as with **depuis**, preposition, above.

▶ For further information on **depuis que** see pp. 17 and 21.

■ Conjunction expressing reason: **puisque**

> **puisqu'il est si impoli je ne lui parle plus**, *since he's so rude I don't speak to him any more*

SOON AND LATE

Soon, early

■ *soon*: **bientôt**

> **on sera bientôt là**, *we'll soon be there*

■ *soon = early*: **tôt**

> **on est arrivé beaucoup trop tôt**, *we got there much too soon (early)*

■ *early = in good time*: **de bonne heure**

> **on est arrivé de bonne heure**, *we got there early*

■ *sooner = earlier*: **plus tôt**

> **nous sommes arrivés plus tôt qu'eux**, *we arrived sooner (earlier) than they did*

■ *sooner* = *in preference*; *rather*: **plutôt**

> **plutôt lui que moi**, *sooner him than me*

Late

■ *late*, time of day: **tard**

> **il est très tard, rentrons**, *it's very late, let's go home*

■ *late*, = *after the appropriate time*: **tard**

> **maintenant il est trop tard**, *now it's too late*

■ *late*, referring to people: **en retard**

> **nous sommes en retard**, *we're late*

■ *late*, adjective: **tardif**

> **à cette heure tardive**, *at this late hour*

■ *late*, adjective, = *dead*: **feu**

> **le tombeau de feu son père**, *his late father's grave*

Feu is invariable. Note its position.

TIME(S)

■ *time(s)* = *occasion(s)*: **la/les fois**

> **pour la première fois**, *for the first time*

■ *time* = *length, amount of time*: **le temps**

> **malheureusement je n'ai pas le temps**, *unfortunately I haven't got (the) time*

■ *time* = *point in time*: **le moment**

> **tu es arrivé au bon moment?**, *you got there at the right moment?*

On time is **à l'heure**; *in (the nick of) time* is **à temps**:

> **tu dois arriver à l'heure**, *you must get there on time*
> **tu es arrivé juste à temps**, *you got there just in time*

■ *time = time of day*: **l'heure**

> **vous avez l'heure?**, *do you have the (right) time?*

■ *time = period*: **l'époque**

> **à cette époque j'étais toujours au lycée**, *at that time I was still at college*

TO BE

To be is translated by verbs other than **être** in the following cases:

■ Location: **se trouver**

> **le garage se trouve derrière la maison**, *the garage is (located) behind the house*

■ Physical states: **avoir**

> **j'ai chaud/froid/faim/soif/sommeil/peur/honte**, *I'm hot/cold/hungry/thirsty/tired/frightened/ashamed*

Similarly: *to be right/wrong* is **avoir raison/tort**.

■ Health: **aller**

> **comment allez-vous?**, *how are you?*
> **maman va beaucoup mieux**, *mother's much better*

■ Weather: **faire**

> **il fait chaud/froid/beau/mauvais/du vent/du brouillard**, *it's hot/cold/fine/bad/windy/foggy*

■ Age: **avoir**

> **elle a vingt et un ans**, *she's twenty-one (years old)*

▶ *I am to/I was to* is translated by **devoir**. See p. 65.

VERB + OBJECT + INFINITIVE

Sentences such as *I want her to go*, *I like her to talk* cannot be translated directly into French, as, with the exception of a very few verbs (see below), this verb + object + infinitive construction does not exist in French. A clause has to be used instead:

> **je veux qu'elle parte**, *I want her to go* ('*I want that she should go*')
>
> **j'aime qu'il me gratte le dos**, *I like him to scratch my back* ('*I like that he scratches my back*')

Both **vouloir que** and **aimer que** in the above examples take the subjunctive.

A similar construction used in English with verbs of perception consists of verb + object + infinitive/present participle (*I hear him speak/speaking*). This construction, with verbs of perception (**voir**, **entendre**, **sentir**, etc.), can be translated directly into French. A dependent infinitive is used:

> **je l'entends parler**, *I hear him speak(ing)*

▶ For further details see p. 42 (subjunctive) and p. 51 (dependent infinitive)

VERB + PREPOSITION COMBINATIONS

Many English verbs consist of a simple verb plus a preposition (*cry out*, *run away*, *run back*). This verb-plus-preposition construction is impossible in French and such verbs, sometimes called phrasal verbs, have to be translated in one of the following ways.

■ By a simple verb:

> **crispée de douleur, elle commença à crier**, *contorted with pain, she began to cry out* (*cry out*: **crier**)

> **à la nuit tombante ils se sont enfuis**, *at nightfall
> they ran away* (*run away*: **s'enfuir**)

■ By a verb based on the preposition, plus a dependent
present participle (with **en**) or an adverb phrase:

> **ils sont retournés en courant**, *they ran back* (*run
> back*: **retourner en courant**, *'go back running'*)
> **ils sont partis à la hâte**, *they hurried off* (*hurry off*:
> **partir à la hâte**, *'go off in a hurry'*)

▶ For further details see p. 36.

■ Where the verb-phrase has an object, by a verb with a
dependent infinitive:

> **laisse-le entrer!**, *let him in*

Several of these are based on **faire**:

> **faire entrer**, *show in*
> **faire sortir**, *show out*
> **faire venir**, *send for*

▶ See p. 73 for more details.

WHATEVER, WHOEVER

Whatever

■ Pronoun subject: **quoi que ce soit qui**; pronoun
object: **quoi que** (both + subjunctive)

> **quoi que ce soit qui bouge, ne tirez pas!**, *whatever
> moves, don't shoot*
> **quoi que ce soit qui ronge votre parquet, ce ne
> sont pas des souris**, *whatever is eating your
> floorboards, it isn't mice*
> **quoi qu'il dise, je ne le crois pas**, *whatever he
> says* (*may say*), *I don't believe him*

■ Adjective: **quel que soit**

> **quel que soit la somme qu'on vous offre**, *whatever money you are offered*
>
> **ne renoncez pas, quelles que soient les difficultés**, *don't give up, whatever the difficulties may be*

■ *Anything whatever* is **quoi que ce soit**, used as if it were a pronoun:

> **il ne se plaint pas de quoi que ce soit**, *he doesn't complain about anything whatever (anything at all)*

Whoever

■ **Qui que ce soit qui** (subject), **qui que ce soit que** (object) both + subjunctive:

> **qui que ce soit qui vous ait dit cela, c'est complètement faux**, *whoever told you that, it's completely untrue*
>
> **qui que ce soit qu'on propose comme candidat, je ne voterai pas**, *whoever they put up as candidate, I shall not vote*

Quiconque may be used (without the subjunctive), in rather more formal style, for **qui que ce soit qui/que**. See p. 130.

| Pronunciation Traps

To attempt to present the pronunciation of French as a whole in a grammar of this kind would be impossible and pointless. It is, however, useful to provide reference to those commonly used words whose pronunciation does not follow the usual patterns or with which learners consistently find pronunciation problems.

The following list gives such problem words alphabetically, with a very approximate imitated pronunciation followed by the exact pronunciation represented by the letters of the International Phonetic Alphabet. In general, related words show the same pronunciation changes (so **le sculpteur**, *sculptor*, is pronounced without a p, like **la sculpture**, listed below).

ail (m.), *garlic*	eye	aj
aile (f.), *wing*	el	ɛl
alcool (m.), *alcohol*	al-col (one o pronounced)	alkɔl
amener, *bring*	am-nay	amne
Amiens (the town)	am-ya	amjɛ̃
automne (m.), *autumn*	oh-tonn (m not pronounced)	otɔn
but, **automnal**, *autumnal*	oh-tom-nal (m often pronounced)	otɔmnal
bœuf (m.), *beef; ox*	berf	bœf
but plural **bœufs**, *cattle; oxen*	berh	bø
cent un, *101*; **cent onze** *111*	son-ern; son-onz (t not pronounced)	sɑ̃ œ̃; sɑ̃ ɔ̃:z
chef (m.), chief, *head*	shef	ʃɛf
but, **chef d'œuvre**, *masterpiece*	shed-er-vr (f not pronounced)	ʃɛdœ̃:vr̥

Christ (m.), *Christ*	creased (t pronounced)	krist
but **Jésus Christ**	jay-zoo-cree (t not pronounced)	ʒezy kri
condamner, *condemn*	con-da-nay (m not pronounced)	kɔ̃dɑne
cuiller (also spelled **cuillère**), (f.) *spoon*	kwee-yair (r pronounced)	kɥijɛːr
dix, *10* (standing alone)	deese	dis
(before a consonant)	dee	di
(before a vowel)	deez	diz
dot, (f.) *dowry*	dot (t pronounced)	dɔt
emmener, *take away*	om-nay	ɑ̃mne
estomac (m.), *stomach*	esto-ma (c not pronounced)	ɛstɔma
eu, *had* (past participle of **avoir**)	ee (+ rounded lips)	y
fier, *proud*	fee-air (r pronounced)	fjɛːr
fils (m.), *son*	feese (s pronounced)	fis
but **fils** (m. pl.), *wires*	feel (s not pronounced)	fil
hais, hait, *hate(s)* (**je**, **tu** and **il** form of present, **haïr**)	eh (i not pronounced separately)	ɛ
hélas, *alas*	ay-lars (s pronounced)	elɑːs
jus (m.), *juice*	joo (s not pronounced)	ʒy
mademoiselle (f.), *miss*	mad-mwa-zel (first e not pronounced)	madmwazɛl
mille, *thousand*	meal (ll pronounced l)	mil

mœurs, (f. pl.), *manners*	merse (s usually pronounced)	mœrs
naïveté (f.), *naïvety*	na-eev-tay	naivte
neuf, *9*	nerf	nœf
but **neuf heures**	ner-vur	nœv œ:r
and **neuf ans**	ner-von (f pronounced v)	nœv ã
notre, *our*; **votre**, *your*	notr; votr	nɔtr̩; vɔtr̩
but, **nôtre**, *ours*; **vôtre**, *yours*	note-r, vote-r (o lengthened)	no:tr̩; vo:tr̩
œuf (m.), *egg*	erf	œf
but plural **œufs**, *eggs*	erh (fs not pronounced, vowel lengthened)	φ
oignon (m.), *onion*	on-yon	ɔɲɔ̃
os (m.), *bone*	os	ɔs
but plural **os**, *bones*	oh (s not pronounced, vowel lengthened)	o
poêle (m.), *stove*; (f.), *frying pan*	pwal	pwal
Reims, (*Rheims*, the town)	ranse	rɛ̃:s
rhum (m.), *rum* and **Rome**, *Rome*	rom	rɔm
sandwich (m.), *sandwich*	*sond-witch*	sãdwitʃ
sceptique, *sceptical*	sep-teek (c not pronounced)	sɛptik
sculpture (f.), *sculpture*	skill-tour (p not pronounced)	skylty:r
sens (m.), *sense*; *direction*	sonse (last s pronounced)	sã:s

six, *6* (standing alone)	cease	sis
(before a consonant)	sea	si
(before a vowel)	seas	siz
solennel, *solemn*	sol-a-nel	sɔlanɛl
	(first e pronounced a)	
tabac (m.),	ta-ba	taba
tobacco(nist's)	(c not pronounced)	
tiers (m.), *third*	tea-air	tjɛːr
	(s not pronounced)	
vieille (f.), *old*	vyay	vjɛːj
but **veille** (f.), *the day*	vay	vɛːj
before		
village (m.), *village*	vee-large	vilaːʒ
	(ll pronounced l)	
ville (f.), *town*	veel	vil
	(ll pronounced l)	
vingt, *20*	van	vɛ̃
but **vingt et un**, *21*	van-tay-ern	vɛ̃t e œ̃
vingt-deux, *22*, etc.	vant-der	vɛ̃t dø
	(t usually pronounced	
	from 21 on)	
wagon (m.), *carriage*	va-gon	vagɔ̃

Verb Tables

▶ See also pp. 7 and 8.

■ Verbs with infinitives ending -**e**[consonant]**er**:

☐ changing the -**e** to -**è** before a mute or unstressed **e**.
See p. 7 for a list of verbs in this group. Model: **acheter**, *to buy*:

present		past participle
j'achète	nous achetons	acheté
tu achètes	vous achetez	
il achète	ils achètent	

future	past historic
j'achèterai	j'achetai

☐ doubling the consonant before a mute or unstressed
-**e**. Model: **jeter**, *to throw*:

present		past participle
je jette	nous jetons	jeté
tu jettes	vous jetez	
il jette	ils jettent	

future	past historic
je jetterai	je jetai

■ Verbs with infinitives ending -é[consonant]er:

The **é** changes to **è** before a mute **e**, but not in the future or conditional. Model: **préférer**, *to prefer*:

present		past participle
je préfère	**nous préférons**	**préféré**
tu préfères	**vous préférez**	
il préfère	**ils préfèrent**	

future	past historic
je préférerai	**je préférai**

■ Verbs with infinitives ending -yer:

The **y** changes to **i** before a mute or unstressed **e**. The change is optional with **-ayer** verbs. Model: **appuyer**, *to lean*:

present		past participle
j'appuie	**nous appuyons**	**appuyé**
tu appuies	**vous appuyez**	
il appuie	**ils appuient**	

future	past historic
j'appuierai	**j'appuyai**

■ Verbs with infinitives ending -cer:

The **c** changes to **ç** before **a** and **o**. Model: **commencer**, *to begin*:

present		past participle
je commence	**nous commençons**	**commencé**
tu commences	**vous commencez**	
il commence	**ils commencent**	

future		past historic
je commencerai		**je commençai**

present participle	imperfect	
commençant	**je commençais**	**nous commencions**
	tu commençais	**vous commenciez**
	il commençait	**ils commençaient**

■ Verbs with infinitives ending **-ger**:

The **g** changes to **ge** before **a** and **o**. Model: **manger**, *to eat*:

present		past participle
je mange	**nous mangeons**	**mangé**
tu manges	**vous mangez**	
il mange	**ils mangent**	

future		past historic
je mangerai		**je mangeai**

present participle	imperfect	
mangeant	**je mangeais**	**nous mangions**
	tu mangeais	**vous mangiez**
	il mangeait	**ils mangeaient**

IRREGULAR VERBS

Verbs, including common compound verbs, are in alphabetical order. Verbs marked * are less common: some parts of these verbs are very rarely met.

Verbs marked † form their compound tenses with **être**.

The parts given are the infinitive, the full present tense, the past participle (from which all compound tenses may be formed, see p. 3), the **je** form of the future (from which the rest of the future and the conditional may be formed), and the **je** form of the past historic (from which the rest of the past historic may be formed). The endings for these last three tenses are:

	future	*conditional*	*past historic*		
je	-ai	-ais	-ai	-is	-us
tu	-as	-ais	-as	-is	-us
il	-a	-ait	-a	-it	-ut
nous	-ons	-ions	-âmes	-îmes	-ûmes
vous	-ez	-iez	-âtes	-îtes	-ûtes
ils	-ont	-aient	-èrent	-irent	-urent

The conditional endings are added to the future stem to form the conditional; the same endings are added to the **nous** form of the present (without its **-ons**) to form the imperfect.

For the formation of the present and imperfect subjunctive see pp. 40 and 41.

infinitive; present	past participle	future	past historic
*acquérir *acquire*			
j'acquiers	acquis	j'acquerrai	j'acquis
tu acquiers			
il acquiert			
nous acquérons			
vous acquérez			
ils acquièrent			

accueillir, *welcome* → **cueillir**

admettre, *admit* → **mettre**

aller† *go*			
je vais	allé	j'irai	j'allai
tu vas			
il va			
nous allons			
vous allez			
ils vont			
pres. subjunctive: **j'aille, nous allions**			

apercevoir, *catch sight of* → **recevoir**

apparaître, *appear* → **connaître**

apprendre, *learn* → **prendre**

infinitive; present	past participle	future	past historic
s'asseoir† *sit down*			
je m'assieds	assis	je m'assiérai	je m'assis
tu t'assieds			
il s'assied			
nous nous asseyons			
vous vous asseyez			
ils s'asseyent			

more colloquial form of present: **je m'assois, tu t'assois, il s'assoit, nous nous assoyons, vous vous assoyez, ils s'assoient**

---

atteindre, *reach* → **peindre**

---

avoir *have*			
j'ai	eu	j'aurai	j'eus
tu as			
il a			
nous avons			
vous avez			
ils ont			

pres. subjunctive: **j'aie, nous ayons**, pres. participle: **ayant**, imperative: **aie, ayons, ayez**

---

*battre *beat*	regular except present: **je bats, tu bats, il bat, nous battons, vous battez, ils battent**

---

*se battre†, *fight* → **battre**

infinitive; present	past participle	future	past historic
boire *drink*			
je bois **tu bois** **il boit** **nous buvons** **vous buvez** **ils boivent**	**bu**	**je boirai**	**je bus**

*bouillir regular except present: **je bous, tu bous, il bout,**
  boil   **nous bouillons, vous bouillez, ils bouillent**

* combattre, *combat* → **battre**

commettre, *commit* → **mettre**

comprendre, *understand* → **prendre**

* concevoir, *conceive* → **recevoir**

infinitive; present	past participle	future	past historic
conduire *drive*			
je conduis **tu conduis** **il conduit** **nous conduisons** **vous conduisez** **ils conduisent**	**conduit**	**je conduirai**	**je conduisis**
connaître *know*			
je connais **tu connais** **il connaît** **nous connaissons** **vous connaissez** **ils connaissent**	**connu**	**je connaîtrai**	**je connus**

infinitive; present	past participle	future	past historic

construire, *construct* → **conduire**

* contraindre, *restrict* → **peindre**

* contredire, *contradict* → **dire** (present: **vous contredisez**)

* convaincre, *convince* → **vaincre**

* coudre
sew

je couds	cousu	je coudrai	je cousis
tu couds			
il coud			
nous cousons			
vous cousez			
ils cousent			

courir
run

je cours	couru	je courrai	je courus
tu cours			
il court			
nous courons			
vous courez			
ils courent			

couvrir
cover

je couvre	couvert	je couvrirai	je couvris
tu couvres			
il couvre			
nous couvrons			
vous couvrez			
ils couvrent			

craindre, *fear* → **peindre**

infinitive; present	past participle	future	past historic
croire *believe*			
je crois tu crois il croit nous croyons vous croyez ils croient	cru	je croirai	je crus
* croître *grow*			
je croîs tu croîs il croît nous croissons vous croissez ils croissent	crû (f.: crue)	je croîtrai	past hist. not used
* cueillir *gather*			
je cueille tu cueilles il cueille nous cueillons vous cueillez ils cueillent	cueilli	je cueillerai	je cueillis
* cuire, *cook* → **conduire**			
décevoir, *deceive* → **recevoir**			
découvrir, *discover* → **couvrir**			
décrire, *describe* → **écrire**			
* détruire, *destroy* → **conduire**			

infinitive; present	past participle	future	past historic
devoir			
must; _owe_			
je dois	**dû**	**je devrai**	**je dus**
tu dois	(f.: **due**,		
il doit	m. pl.: **dus**,		
nous devons	f. pl.: **dues**)		
vous devez			
ils doivent			
dire			
say			
je dis	**dit**	**je dirai**	**je dis**
tu dis			
il dit			
nous disons			
vous dites			
ils disent			

dormir, _sleep_ → **partir**

infinitive; present	past participle	future	past historic
écrire			
write			
j'écris	**écrit**	**j'écrirai**	**j'écrivis**
tu écris			
il écrit			
nous écrivons			
vous écrivez			
ils écrivent			

* **élire**, _elect_ → **lire**

* **émouvoir**, _move_; _stir up_ → **mouvoir** (past participle: **ému**)

* **s'enquérir†**, _enquire_ → **acquérir**

infinitive; present	past participle	future	past historic
envoyer *send*			
j'envoie	**envoyé**	**j'enverrai**	**j'envoyai**
tu envoies			
il envoie			
nous envoyons			
vous envoyez			
ils envoient			

éteindre, *switch off*; *put out* → **peindre**

être *be*			
je suis	**été**	**je serai**	**je fus**
tu es			
il est			
nous sommes			
vous êtes			
ils sont			

pres. subjunctive: **je sois, nous soyons,**
pres. participle: **étant**, imperative: **sois, soyons, soyez**

* **étreindre**, *embrace* → **peindre**

faire *do*; *make*			
je fais			
tu fais	**fait**	**je ferai**	**je fis**
il fait			
nous faisons			
vous faites			
ils font			

pres. subjunctive: **je fasse, nous fassions**

infinitive; present	past participle	future	past historic
falloir *must*; *be necessary*			
il faut	**fallu**	**il faudra**	**il fallut**
pres. subjunctive: **il faille**			
* fuir *flee*			
je fuis	**fui**	**je fuirai**	**je fuis**
tu fuis			
il fuit			
nous fuyons			
vous fuyez			
ils fuient			
* haïr *hate*			
je hais	**haï**	**je haïrai**	**je haïs**
tu hais			
il hait			
nous haïssons			
vous haïssez			
ils haïssent			
(past. historic: **nous haïmes**, **vous haïtes**, imperfect subjunctive: **il haït**—but all three forms are virtually unused)			

* s'inscrire†, *have oneself registered* → **écrire**

interdire, *forbid* → **dire** (present: **vous interdisez**)

introduire, *introduce*; *put in* → **conduire**

joindre, *join* → **peindre**

infinitive; present	past participle	future	past historic
lire *read*			
je lis	**lu**	**je lirai**	**je lus**
tu lis			
il lit			
nous lisons			
vous lisez			
ils lisent			
*luire *shine*			
il luit	**lui**	**il luira**	past hist.
ils luisent	(no f.)		not used
mentir, *tell lies* → **partir**			
mettre *put*			
je mets	**mis**	**je mettrai**	**je mis**
tu mets			
il met			
nous mettons			
vous mettez			
ils mettent			
*moudre *grind*			
je mouds	**moulu**	**je moudrai**	**je moulus**
tu mouds			
il moud			
nous moulons			
vous moulez			
ils moulent			

infinitive; present	past participle	future	past historic
mourir† *die*			
je meurs	**mort**	**je mourrai**	**je mourus**
tu meurs			
il meurt			
nous mourons			
vous mourez			
ils meurent			
* mouvoir *drive*; *propel*			
je meus	**mû**	**je mouvrai**	**je mus**
tu meus	(f. **mue**)		(rare)
il meut			
nous mouvons			
vous mouvez			
ils meuvent			

* naître†, *be born* → **connaître** (past participle: **né**, past historic: **je naquis**)

* nuire, *harm* → **cuire** (past participle: **nui**)

offrir, *offer* → **couvrir**

ouvrir, *open* → **couvrir**

* paître, *graze* → **connaître** (no past participle or past historic)

paraître, *appear* → **connaître**

infinitive; present	past participle	future	past historic
partir† *leave*			
je pars	**parti**	**je partirai**	**je partis**
tu pars			
il part			
nous partons			
vous partez			
ils partent			
peindre *paint*			
je peins	**peint**	**je peindrai**	**je peignis**
tu peins			
il peint			
nous peignons			
vous peignez			
ils peignent			

* plaindre, *pity* → **peindre**

* plaire *please*			
je plais	**plu**	**je plairai**	**je plus**
tu plais			
il plaît			
nous plaisons			
vous plaisez			
ils plaisent			

pleuvoir *rain*			
il pleut	**plu**	**il pleuvra**	**il plut**
pres. subjunctive: **il pleuve**			

poursuivre, *pursue* → **suivre**

infinitive; present	past participle	future	past historic
pouvoir *can; be able*			
je peux (puis-je?)	**pu**	**je pourrai**	**je pus**
tu peux			
il peut			
nous pouvons			
vous pouvez			
ils peuvent			
pres. subjunctive: **je puisse, nous puissions**			
prendre *take*			
je prends	**pris**	**je prendrai**	**je pris**
tu prends			
il prend			
nous prenons			
vous prenez			
ils prennent			
produire, *produce* → **conduire**			
*promouvoir, *promote*: only infinitive and past participle (**promu**) used			
recevoir *receive*			
je reçois	**reçu**	**je recevrai**	**je reçus**
tu reçois			
il reçoit			
nous recevons			
vous recevez			
ils reçoivent			
reconnaître, *recognize* → **connaître**			

infinitive; present	past participle	future	past historic
* réduire, *reduce* → **conduire**			
* se repentir†, *repent* → **partir**			
* résoudre *resolve*			
je **résous**	résolu	je	je **résolus**
tu **résous**		**résoudrai**	
il **résout**			
nous **résolvons**			
vous **résolvez**			
ils **résolvent**			
* restreindre, *restrain; limit* → **peindre**			
rire *laugh*			
je **ris**	ri	je **rirai**	je **ris**
tu **ris**			
il **rit**			
nous **rions**			
vous **riez**			
ils **rient**			
* rompre *break*			
je **romps**	rompu	je **romprai**	je **rompis**
tu **romps**			
il **rompt**			
nous **rompons**			
vous **rompez**			
ils **rompent**			

infinitive; present	past participle	future	past historic

savoir
know

je sais	su	je saurai	je sus

tu sais
il sait
nous savons
vous savez
ils savent

pres. subjunctive: **je sache, nous sachions**
pres. participle: **sachant**; used as adjective, **savant**
imperative: **sache, sachons, sachez**

---

* séduire, *seduce* → **conduire**

---

sentir, se sentir†, *feel* → **partir**

---

servir, *serve* → **partir**

---

sortir†, *go out* → **partir**

---

souffrir, *suffer* → **couvrir**

---

sourire, *smile* → **rire**

---

suffire, *be (quite) enough* → **lire**   (past participle: **suffi**, past historic: **je suffis**)

---

suivre
follow

je suis	suivi	je suivrai	je suivis

tu suis
il suit
nous suivons
vous suivez
ils suivent

---

surprendre, *surprise* → **prendre**

---

* survivre, *survive* → **vivre**

infinitive; present	past participle	future	past historic

* se taire†, *be quiet* → **plaire** (present: **il se tait**)

tenir, *hold* → **venir**

traduire, *translate* → **conduire**

* vaincre
  defeat

je vaincs	vaincu	je vaincrai	je vainquis
tu vaincs			
il vainc			
nous vainquons			
vous vainquez			
ils vainquent			

* valoir
  be worth

je vaux	valu	je vaudrai	je valus
tu vaux			
il vaut			
nous valons			
vous valez			
ils valent			

pres. subjunctive: **je vaille, nous valions, ils vaillent**; forms other than **il** extremely uncommon in all tenses

venir†
  come

je viens	venu	je viendrai	je vins
tu viens			tu vins
il vient			il vint
nous venons			nous vînmes
vous venez			vous vîntes
ils viennent			ils vinrent

infinitive; present	past participle	future	past historic

* vêtir
  dress

je vêts	vêtu	je vêtirai	je vêtis
tu vêts			
il vêt			
nous vêtons			
vous vêtez			
ils vêtent			

(present **nous vêtissons, vous vêtissez, ils vêtissent,** present part. **vêtissant,** and imperfect **je vêtissais** etc. are also found)

vivre
  live

je vis	vécu	je vivrai	je vécus
tu vis			
il vit			
nous vivons			
vous vivez			
ils vivent			

voir
  see

je vois	vu	je verrai	je vis
tu vois			
il voit			
nous voyons			
vous voyez			
ils voient			

infinitive; present	past participle	future	past historic
vouloir			
want			
je veux	**voulu**	**je voudrai**	**je voulus**
tu veux			
il veut			
nous voulons			
vous voulez			
ils veulent			

pres. subjunctive: **je veuille, nous voulions**
imperative: **veuille, veuillez** (= *would you kindly*)

Glossary of Grammatical Terms

Abstract Noun The name of something that is not a concrete object or person. Words such as *difficulty, hope, discussion* are abstract nouns.

Active See Passive.

Adjective A word describing a noun. *A big, blue, untidy painting*—*big, blue, untidy* are adjectives describing the noun *painting*.

Adverb A word that describes or modifies (i) a verb: *he did it gracefully* (adverb: *gracefully*), or (ii) an adjective: *a disgracefully large helping* (adverb: *disgracefully*), or (iii) another adverb: *she skated extraordinarily gracefully* (adverbs: *extraordinarily, gracefully*).

Agreement In French, adjectives agree with nouns, verbs agree with subject nouns or pronouns, pronouns agree with nouns, etc. This is a way of showing that something refers to or goes with something else. Agreement is by number (showing whether something is singular or plural) and by gender (showing whether something is masculine or feminine). For instance: **des chaussettes bleues**, *blue socks*: **-e** is added to the adjective because **chaussette** is feminine, **-s** is added to **bleue** because **chaussettes** is plural.

Apposition Two nouns or noun phrases are used together, the second one explaining the first: *the station master, a big man with a moustache, came in.* 'A big man with a moustache' is in apposition to 'the station master'.

Articles The little words like *a* and *the* that stand in front of nouns. In English, *the* is the definite article (it defines a particular item in a category: *the hat you've got on*); *a* or *an* is the indefinite article (it doesn't specify which item in a category: *wear a hat, any hat*); *some* is the partitive article (it specifies a part but not the whole of a category: *I'd like some mustard*).

Attributive Noun A noun used as an adjective: *a petrol pump*: 'petrol' is an attributive noun, telling us what sort of pump.

Auxiliary Verb A verb used to help form a compound tense. In *I am walking, he has walked* the auxiliary verbs are *to be* (*am*) and *to have* (*has*).

Cardinal Numbers The numbers used in counting (*one, two, three, four*, etc.). Compare with Ordinal Numbers.

Clause A self-contained section of a sentence containing a verb: *He came in and was opening his mail when the lights went out*—'he came in', 'and (he) was opening his mail', 'when the lights went out' are clauses.

Comparative With adjectives and adverbs, the form produced by adding *-er* or prefixing *more*: *bigger, more difficult, more easily*.

Compound Noun Noun formed from two or more separate words, usually hyphenated in French: **le tire-bou-chon**, *corkscrew*—both English and French words are compound nouns.

Compound Tense Tense of a verb formed by a part of that verb preceded by an auxiliary verb (*am, have, shall*, etc.): *am walking; have walked; shall walk*.

Compound Verb Verb formed by the addition of a prefix (*un-, over-, de-, dis-*, etc.) to another verb: simple verbs: *wind, take*; compound verbs: *unwind, overtake*.

Conditional Perfect Tense The tense used to express what might have happened (if something else had occurred) and formed in English with *should have* (*I* *should have walked, we should have walked*) or *would have* (*you would have walked, he would have walked, they would have walked*).

Conditional Tense The tense used to express what might happen (if something else occurred) and formed in English with *should* (*I should walk, we should walk*) or *would* (*you would walk, he would walk, they would walk*).

Conjugation The pattern which a type of verb follows. There is only one regular conjugation in English: *to walk*: present, *I walk, he walks*; past, *he walked*; perfect, *he has walked*, etc.

Conjunction A word like *and, but, when, because* that starts a clause and joins it to the rest of the sentence.

Consonant A letter representing a sound that can only be used in conjunction with a vowel. In French, the vowels are **a, e, i, o, u, y**. All the other letters of the alphabet are consonants.

Definite Article See Articles.

Demonstrative Adjective An adjective that is used to point out a particular thing: *I'll have that cake; this cake is terrible; give me those cakes*—*that, this, those* are demonstrative adjectives.

Demonstrative Article Alternative name for Demonstrative Adjective.

Demonstrative Pronoun A pronoun that is used to point out a particular thing: *I'll have that; this is terrible; give me those*—*that, this, those* are demonstrative pronouns.

Direct Object The noun or pronoun that experiences the action of the verb: *he hits me*, direct object: *me*. See also Indirect Object.

Disjunctive Pronoun Also called Stressed Pronoun. A pronoun that does not stand directly with a verb as its subject or object: *Who said that? Me!*—*me* is a disjunctive pronoun. Disjunctives in French have different forms from ordinary personal pronouns.

Ending See Stem.

Feminine See Gender.

First Conjugation Verb In French, a verb whose infinitive ends in **-er**.

First Person See Third Person.

Future Perfect Tense The tense used to express what, at some future time, will be a past occurrence. Formed in English with *shall have* (*I shall have walked, we shall have walked*) and *will have* (*you will have walked, he will have walked, they will have walked*).

Future Tense The tense used to express a future occurrence and formed in English with *shall* (*I shall walk, we shall walk*) or *will* (*you will walk, he will walk, they will walk*).

Gender In French, a noun or pronoun may be either masculine or feminine: this is known as the gender of the noun or pronoun. The gender may correspond to the sex of the thing named, or may not. In English gender only shows in pronouns (*he, she, it*, etc.) and corresponds to the sex of the thing named. See Agreement.

Historic Present Present tense used to relate past events, often in order to make the narrative more vivid: *So then I go into the kitchen and what do I see?*

Imperative The form of the verb that expresses a command. In English it is usually the same as the infinitive without *to*: infinitive, *to walk*, imperative, *walk!*

Imperfect Subjunctive One of the past tenses of the French subjunctive. See Subjunctive.

Imperfect Tense A French past tense formed by adding a set of endings (**-ais, -ais, -ait**, etc.) to the **nous** form of the present tense minus its **-ons**. Often corresponds to the English past continuous: **je marchais**, *I was walking*.

Impersonal Verb A verb whose subject is an imprecise *it* or *there*: *it is raining*; *there's no need for that*.

Indefinite Adjectives Adjectives such as *each, such, some, other, every, several*.

Indefinite Article See Articles.

Indefinite Pronouns Pronouns such as *somebody, anybody, something, anything, everybody, nobody*.

Indirect Object The noun or pronoun at which the direct object is aimed. In English it either has or can have *to* in front of it: *I passed it (to) him*, indirect object *(to) him*; *I gave her my address (I gave my address to her)*, indirect object *(to) her*. In these examples *it* and *my address* are direct objects. See Direct Object.

Indirect Question A question (without a question mark) in a subordinate clause. It is introduced by some such expression as *I wonder if, do you know where, I'll tell him when*. Direct question: *When is he coming?* Indirect question: *I don't know when he's coming*.

Infinitive The basic part of the verb from which other parts are derived. In English, it is normally preceded by *to*: *to walk, to run*.

Interrogative The question form of the verb.

Interrogative Adjective A question word (in English *which ...?* or *what ...?*) used adjectivally with a following noun: *which book do you mean?*

Interrogative Adverb An adverb that introduces a direct question, in English *why?, when?, how?*, etc. In indirect questions the same words function as conjunctions, joining the question to the main clause. *Why do you say that?*—direct question, *why* is an interrogative adverb; *I don't know why you say that*—indirect question, *why* is a conjunction.

Interrogative Pronoun A pronoun that asks a question, in English *who?* and *what?*

Intransitive Of verbs: having no direct object.

Irregular Verb In French, a verb that does not follow the pattern of one of the three regular conjugations.

Main Clause A clause within a sentence that could stand on its own and still make sense. For example: *He came in when he was ready. He came in* is a main clause (it makes sense standing on its own); *when he was ready* is a subordinate clause (it can't stand on its own and still make sense).

Masculine See Gender.

Modal Verbs (literally 'verbs of mood') These are the auxiliary verbs (other than *have* and *be*) that always appear with a dependent infinitive: *I can walk, I must walk, I will walk—can, must, will* are modal verbs.

Noun A word that names a person or thing. *Peter, box, glory, indecision* are nouns.

Noun Clause A clause that is the equivalent of a noun within the sentence: *I don't want to catch whatever you've got* (*whatever you've got* is a clause for which we might substitute a noun, e.g., *measles*).

Number With nouns, pronouns, etc.—the state of being either singular or plural. See Agreement.

Object See Direct Object and Indirect Object.

Ordinal (Number) A number such as *first, second, third, fourth,* normally used adjectivally about one thing in a series.

Partitive Article See Articles.

Passive The basic tenses of a verb are active. Passive tenses are the set of tenses that are used in order to make the person or thing experiencing the action of the verb (normally the object) into the subject of the verb. Active (basic tense): *I discover it*, passive: *it is discovered (by me)*; active: *he ate them*, passive: *they were eaten (by him)*.

Past Anterior Tense A French tense equivalent in time to the pluperfect, formed with the past historic of **avoir** or **être** + past participle: **j'eus marché**, *I had walked*.

Past Historic Tense A French past tense used in writing narrative instead of the perfect; often eqivalent to the English simple past tense: **je marchai**, *I walked*.

Past Participle The part of the verb used to form compound past tenses. In English, it usually ends in -*ed*; verb: *to walk*; past participle: *walked*; perfect tense: *I have walked*.

Perfect Continuous In English, the past tense formed using *was* + -*ing*, implying that something was continuing to occur: *I was walking*.

Perfect Infinitive The past form of the infinitive, formed in English from *to have* + past participle: *to have walked*.

Perfect Participle The part of the verb that in English is formed by *having* + past participle: *having walked away, he now came back*: *having walked* is a perfect participle.

Perfect Tense The past tense that, in English, is formed by using *have* + past participle: *I have walked*.

Personal Pronouns Subject and object pronouns referring to people or things (*he, him, she, her, it*, etc.).

Phrasal Verb In English, a verb made by combining a simple verb with a preposition: *run out, jump up, stand down*.

Phrase A self-contained section of a sentence that does not contain a full verb. *Being late as usual, he arrived at* *a quarter past eleven*: *at a quarter past eleven* is a phrase; present and past participles are not full verbs, so *being late as usual* is also a phrase. Compare Clause.

Pluperfect Continuous In English, the equivalent tense to the pluperfect using *had been + -ing*, implying that something had been going on (when something else happened), e.g.: *I had been walking for an hour, when ...*

Pluperfect Tense The past tense, that, in English, is formed by using *had* + past participle: *I had walked.*

Possessive Adjective An adjective that indicates possession; in English, *my, your, her*, etc.: *that is my book.*

Possessive Article Alternative name for Possessive Adjective.

Possessive Pronoun A pronoun that indicates possession; in English, *mine, yours, hers*, etc.: *that book is mine.*

Preposition A word like *in, over, near, across* that stands in front of a noun or pronoun relating it to the rest of the sentence.

Present Continuous See Present Tense.

Present Participle The part of the verb that in English ends in *-ing*: *to walk*: present participle, *walking.*

Present Tense The tense of the verb that refers to things now happening regularly (simple present: *I walk*), or happening at the moment (present continuous: *I am walking*).

Pronoun A word such as *he, she, which, mine* that stands instead of a noun (usually already mentioned).

Reflexive Verbs Verbs whose object is the same as their subject: *he likes himself, she can dress herself. Himself, herself* are reflexive pronouns.

Relative Pronoun A pronoun that introduces a subordinate clause and at the same time allows that clause to function as an adjective or noun. In English the relative pronouns are *who(m)*, *which*, *whose*, *that*, and *what*. *Tell me what you know!*: *what you know* is a noun clause and the direct object of *tell me*. It is introduced by the relative pronoun *what*. *That's the lad who stole my wallet*: *who stole my wallet* is an adjectival clause describing *lad*. It is introduced by the relative pronoun *who*.

Second Conjugation Verb In French, a verb whose infinitive ends in **-ir**.

Second Person See Third Person.

Simple Tense A one-word tense of a verb: *I walk*, *I run* (as opposed to a compound tense: *I am walking*, *I was running*).

Stem The part of a verb to which endings indicating tense, person, etc. are added. Verb: *to walk*: stem, *walk-*: *he walk-s*, *he walk-ed*, etc.

Stressed Pronouns See Disjunctive Pronouns.

Subject (of verb, clause, or sentence) The noun or pronoun that initiates the action of the verb: *George walked*, subject: *George*; *he hit George*, subject: *he*.

Subjunctive In French, a set of tenses that express doubt or unlikelihood. The subjunctive still exists in only a few expressions in English: *If I were you* [but I'm not], *I'd go now* (*I were* is subjunctive—the normal past tense is *I was*).

Subordinate Clause A clause in a sentence that depends, in order to make sense, on a main clause. See Main Clause.

Subordinating Conjunction The conjunction that introduces a subordinate clause.

Superlative With adjectives and adverbs, the form produced by adding *-est* or prefixing *most*: *biggest*, *most difficult*, *most easily*.

Tense The form of a verb that indicates when the action takes place (e.g., present tense: *I walk*; past tense: *I walked*).

Third Conjugation Verb In French, a verb whose infinitive ends in **-re**.

Third Person *He, she, it, they* (and their derivatives, like *him, his, her, their*), or any noun. The first person is *I* or *we* (and their derivatives), the second person is *you* (and its derivatives).

Transitive Of verbs: having a direct object.

Verb The word that tells you what the subject of the clause does: *he goes*; *she dislikes me*; *have you eaten it?*, *they know nothing*—*goes, dislikes, have eaten, know* are verbs.

Verbal Noun Part of the verb (in English, usually the present participle) used as a noun: *smoking is bad for you*: verbal noun, *smoking*.

Vowel A letter representing a sound that can be pronounced by itself without the addition of other sounds. In French the vowels are **a, e, i, o, u, y**.

| Index

English prepositions should be looked up in the alphabetical list on page 185.

French prepositions should be looked up in the alphabetical list on page 164.

Irregular verbs should be looked up in the alphabetical list on page 242.

The preposition a verb takes before an infinitive or noun will be found in the alphabetical list of verbs on page 59.

Words offering problems of pronunciation should be looked up in the alphabetical list on page 235.

Definitions of grammatical terms will be found in the glossary on page 260.